They Call Her Pastor

SUNY Series in Religion, Culture, and Society
WADE CLARK ROOF, Editor

THEY CALL HER PASTOR

A New Role for Catholic Women

RUTH A. WALLACE

STATE UNIVERSITY OF NEW YORK PRESS

Published by
State University of New York Press, Albany

© 1992   State University of New York

Printed in the United States of America

For information, address State University of New York
Press, State University Plaza, Albany, N.Y. 12246

Production by Bernadine Dawes
Marketing by Fran Keneston

Library of Congress Cataloging-in-Publication Data

Wallace, Ruth A.
    They call her pastor : a new role for Catholic women / Ruth A.
Wallace.
        p.   cm. — (SUNY series in religion, culture, and society)
    Includes bibliographical references and index.
    ISBN 0–7914–0925–2 (alk. paper) : $44.50. — ISBN 0–7914–0926–0
(pbk. : alk. paper) : $14.95
        1. Women in church work—Catholic Church. 2. Women clergy—United
States.   I. Title. II. Series.
BX2347.8.W6W34   1992
262' . 142' 082—dc20
                                                                91–15121
                                                                    CIP

10 9 8 7 6 5 4 3 2

To the Women Pastors Who Made This Possible

CONTENTS

PREFACE

This book is the result of my study of twenty Catholic parishes administered by women, as seen by the women themselves, their parishioners, and the priests who travel to the parishes to preside at Mass and the other sacraments. Such parishes are often referred to as "priestless parishes" because they are without a resident priest.

I am deeply indebted to these women who allowed me to intrude on their very busy lives. Without their cooperation, and that of their parishioners and priests, this book would not have been possible. Although their names will not appear, they are deeply etched in my memory.

By the time this book goes to press I will have spent the better part of two years working on the research project that is the foundation for these chapters. In addition to the professional gratification resulting from the opportunity to get in on the initial stages of a "cutting-edge" phenomenon, I want to mention briefly some of the personal compensations for the time and energy that I expended on this project.

Chronologically the first reward was the astounding cooperation I received from the women pastors. When I contacted them as potential subjects, they did not know me, and yet all of them agreed to participate in the study. Moreover, most of them invited me to stay with them in their homes when I visited their parishes for the weekend. Even more important, they were so generous with their time for interviewing, touring the parish, and letting me accompany them on their various duties over the weekend, that I came away with data that was not only extremely rich in quality, but also more than enough for a book.

Secondly I had a number of unforgettable encounters in my travels to these parishes. A chance meeting in an airport with the bishop who headed the diocese where one of my parishes was located was one of these. Because he had the power to prohibit me from gathering data in his parishes, this unexpected encounter could have sabotaged the project, had it not been for the quick thinking of a woman pastor, which I describe later in the book.

Some of my most profoundly moving experiences occurred when I accompanied women pastors to visit sick and dying parishioners. I will never forget the loving atmosphere in those rooms that in my view transformed their seemingly bleak living conditions. Likewise, I was enriched culturally time and time again as I took part in community gatherings on such occasions as weddings and wedding receptions, baptisms and baptismal parties, and numerous parish dinners all over the United States. Needless to say, a key ingredient at most of these gatherings was the food, the wonderfully fresh produce from the parishioners' farms, and their delicious home cooking. But the overwhelming reward, in my view, was the opportunity to experience a real spirit of community on these occasions.

Finally, there were also a number of geographical "firsts." Four of the states I had never visited before, and nineteen of the twenty parishes were located in towns or cities that were also new territory for me. The opportunity to observe in person these isolated and relatively poor parishes expanded my understanding of the context of the women pastors' work. These visits to parishes throughout the country also enriched my personal experience of racial and ethnic diversity. I heard accents and singing, watched dancing and experienced camaraderie that were new and refreshing.

I would like to thank the Lilly Endowment for a grant (#890087) that provided the time and the resources for my travel throughout the United States to collect the data, and allowed for the transcription of interviews and other related expenses. I am also grateful to the National Science Foundation for an award (#SES 89–12263) which provided for a graduate student assistant to help in the processing of the data.

There are others whose help at various stages of this study was invaluable to me. In particular, I want to thank Kay Sheskaitis, Kathryn Meadow-Orlans, Jenifer Oberg, James Coriden, Sheila Harvil, Sally Davis, Peter Gilmour, Phillip Murnion, Fred Hofheinz, Phyllis Moen, Helen Kelley, Helen Fuchs Ebaugh, Janet Saltzman Chafetz, Dorothy Smith, Arlie Russell Hochschild, Jacqueline Wiseman, Shirley F. Hartley, Carla Howery, Martin Mangan, and Maureen Healy.

Why Women Pastors?

"A woman in charge of a Catholic parish? You've got to be kidding."

"I can't imagine it in my wildest dreams! You must be talking about something happening on another planet, or at least in another country."

"Well, I can assure you that I've never experienced or heard of such a thing, and I've been a churchgoing Catholic all my life."

These reactions are typical of what I heard over and over again from people who listened as I described my research, a study of women administering priestless parishes in the United States. Many Catholics, particularly those living in the northeastern part of the United States, are unaware of the priest shortage, which is particularly acute in rural areas in the Midwest, the South, and western regions of this country.[1] Though these same Catholics may have heard of dioceses where the bishop has decided to close some parishes because of staffing problems, they were not cognizant of other alternatives like this one, now available to bishops.

Given the patriarchal structure of the Catholic church, and the conservative stance of the current members of the Roman Curia[2] regarding the role of women in the church, one would not expect to see women appointed to significant leadership positions. The women I interviewed have been entrusted by their bishops with the pastoral care of parishes where there are no resident priests. In this capacity these women exercise overall responsibility in the parish for worship, education, pastoral services, and administration.

When, why, and how did it happen that Catholic bishops can appoint lay people, even women, as administrators of priestless parishes? This chapter provides a fourfold answer. First we look at the Second Vatican Council and subsequent changes in church law, and then we turn to the remaining facilitating factors, demographic changes and the contemporary women's movement, before describing my research.

THE IMPACT OF THE SECOND VATICAN COUNCIL

Shortly after Pope John XXIII was elected pope, he expressed his desire to bring about some changes in the church that would allow for better adaptation to modern society, changes which he referred to as *aggiornamento,* an updating or modernization, that would result in an opening of the "windows of the church" to the contemporary world.[3] To that end he convened all Catholic bishops throughout the world for the Second Vatican Council. These council sessions took place in Rome for approximately three months, from September through November, for four consecutive years, beginning in 1962 and ending with the fourth session in 1965.

The central participants in the Vatican Council deliberations from 1962 to 1965 were the 2,540 bishops and a few male heads of religious orders who had voting rights. In addition, there were approximately 450 priests invited as experts (*periti*), and some Protestant observers and representatives from non-Christian religions, all of whom were men.[4] These experts were allowed to be present at the Council deliberations but had no voting rights.

Beginning with the second session of the Council in 1963, a few lay auditors were also invited. By the end of Council deliberations in 1965, there were twelve laywomen, ten religious women, and twenty-seven laymen from different parts of the world present in Rome and participating as auditors.[5] These forty-nine lay auditors were present during the Council deliberations, but they had no vote and they could not speak, except at the various commission meetings held all over Rome. The list of auditors included one woman and two men from the United States: Sister Mary Luke Tobin, the mother general of the Sisters of Loretto, James Norris, and Martin H. Work. There were also a few well-known American Catholic laywomen, such as Dorothy Day, Patricia Crowley, Abigail McCarthy, and Mary Daly, present at peripheral activities, like the noontime Council summary and the daily press briefings on the Council debates. Some women were also present at public talks given occasionally by eminent theologians, and a few women could be seen at occasional weekend conferences and informal gatherings at Roman restaurants.

Some of my personal observations in Rome during the fourth session of the Council in 1965 may be helpful for an understanding of a woman's "place" during the Council.[6] There were many dramatic displays of patriarchal symbolism. An unforgettable sight, for instance, was the daily convergence of hundreds of bishops from all over the world dressed in their colorful regalia at the doors of St. Peter's Church. No layperson could be seen among them because the front entrance was reserved solely for the voting members of the Council. Women who were not auditors participated in the Council itself only by attending the Mass celebrated before each day's Council session. However, they were instructed to leave immediately after the liturgy, because only bishops, *periti,* auditors, and staff could be present for the Council deliberations. (There were some mornings when we felt we were literally being shoved out of St. Peter's, like uninvited guests at a party, because the church ushers pointed to the door while announcing in very loud and insistent voices, *"Exeunt omnes,"* indicating that we were to exit immediately.)

During Council deliberations, the authorized presence of twenty-two women auditors and a total of approximately three thousand men afforded women a very low profile at best. In addition, a woman's voice was *never* heard during the Council deliberations because of the limitations placed on the role of auditor. In general, women were virtually invisible and entirely silent when decisions were made regarding important structural changes affecting all members of the church.[7]

Vatican II Documents and Their Implementation

A perusal of the Vatican II documents reveals that there were only a few instances where any attention was given to the contribution of women to the church. Given the invisibility and silence of women during the Council, it is not surprising that women's issues are seldom addressed in the documents themselves, even in the document on the laity that was supposedly addressed to laywomen and laymen alike.

However, one statement in the document on the laity that was inserted only during the final drafting, reads: "Since in our times women have an ever active share in the whole life of society, it is very important that they participate more widely also in the various fields of the Church's apostolate."[8]

How was this Council statement regarding women's increasing participation implemented? There were some women in important positions before the Second Vatican Council convened in 1962. In fact, looking back historically to the medieval Christian church we can point to abbesses who wielded a considerable amount of power over priests and bishops. Many people will be surprised to learn that some or all of the following rights and duties belonged to abbesses:[9] licensing bishops to exercise pontifical rites in her district; licensing priests to say Mass in her churches; absolving in cases of excommunication; walking in front of the clergy and carrying the pastoral cross in processions; establishing new parishes; holding places in councils with a rank above the clergy; reading the gospel; suspending clergy subject to her; and even, at one time, hearing confessions and preaching in public. It is all the more amazing to realize that this quasi-episcopal status of abbesses did not come to an end until after the French Revolution in the late eighteenth century.[10]

In the period just prior to the convening of Vatican II women could be found in such important positions as administrators of Catholic hospitals, presidents of Catholic women's colleges, and principals of Catholic high schools and grammar schools. However, these were not viewed as strictly "clerical" roles, and the vast majority of women occupying these positions were members of religious communities.[11]

In those sections of the world where bishops and priests

encouraged the laity to participate more actively in the post-Vatican II era, some women gradually assumed more prominent roles. At the parish level they accepted new ministerial roles such as lectors, eucharistic ministers, acolytes (altar servers), and directors of religious education. A study of Catholic parishes in the United States twenty years after the Council found that fifty-two percent of the members of parish councils, sixty percent of eucharistic ministers, and half of the lectors were women.[12] The response of the laity has been largely supportive of this trend. When asked who were the "most influential parishioners," exclusive of the pastors, the respondents produced a list that was fifty-eight percent women.[13]

In our national study of the laity we found that a majority of Catholics think laymen and women should have the right to participate in the following areas which pertain to parish life: deciding how parish income should be spent (eighty percent agreed); giving occasional sermons at Mass (sixty-nine percent agreed); deciding whether to have altar girls (sixty-six percent agreed); being in charge of a parish when the priest is absent (sixty-five percent agreed); and selecting the priests for their parish (fifty-seven percent said they should have this right).[14]

Prior to Vatican II, women were excluded from such roles as students or faculty members in seminaries. It was only after the Vatican Council ended in 1965 that women were admitted to schools of theology for ministerial preparation. Before 1965, then, only those priests who went to college before entering the seminary had the experience of a college education that included women as students and/or teachers. Before the Council ended, most future priests studied for their college degrees in seminaries or schools of theology, where the only women visible were the "good Sisters" who did the cooking, laundering, and other housekeeping tasks. Thus many Catholic priests today, as well as most of the bishops, have had little experience beyond high school in working with women as intellectual equals.

The admission of women students to Roman Catholic schools of theology has resulted in an influx of women ministerial candidates. At the present time, approximately one-fourth of the students enrolled in Roman Catholic theological schools in the United States are women.[15]

Training in theology certainly enhanced a woman's chances of being appointed to positions that were formerly reserved to the clergy, such as superintendents of schools, chancellors of dioceses, canon lawyers, professors in seminaries, directors of Catholic charities, editors of diocesan newspapers, chaplains, spiritual guides and leaders in retreats and Bible studies, and even, as we shall see, as administrators of priestless parishes.[16] Since the percentage of women entering seminaries as students is on an upward trend, we may expect that the daily interaction among these women, their fellow students, and coworkers will have a positive influence on the attitudes and future behavior of these seminarians and priests as they become pastors of parishes and administrators in chancery offices.

Prior to Vatican II, many of the new activities currently assumed by lay people were restricted to the clergy by church law, thus conferring a legitimacy and seeming immutability to the existing structure. We turn now to a discussion of the ensuing revisions of the Code of Canon Law necessitated by the decisions emanating from this historic Council which ultimately sanctioned far-reaching changes, particularly for women's roles in the church.

The New Code of Canon Law

Realizing the importance of changes in church law for the implementation of Vatican Council decisions, Pope John XXIII called for the revision of Canon Law in 1959. The new Code of Canon Law, promulgated in 1983, made some provisions for the expansion of women's roles in the church. While still excluding women from the ordained ministry, the new code opened the following positions to women on the diocesan level: diocesan chancellors, auditors, assessors, defenders of the marriage bond, promoters of justice, judges on diocesan courts, and members of diocesan synods and financial and pastoral councils.

The legal change that opened the door for the recruitment of women as pastoral administrators in priestless parishes can be found in this revised code. In recognition of the priest shortage, the new code included a provision for people other than priests to exercise pastoral care, that is, to perform some of the duties of the pastor in a parish. The new canon (or ruling), 517.2, reads thus:

> If the diocesan bishop should decide that due to a dearth of priests a participation in the exercise of the pastoral care of a parish is to be entrusted to a deacon or to some other person who is not a priest, or to a community of persons, he is to appoint some priest endowed with the power and faculties of a pastor, to supervise the pastoral care.[17]

For women, of course, the inclusionary clause in the wording of canon 517.2 is "some other person who is not a priest," because women cannot be ordained as priests or deacons. This could be viewed as a Pandora's box for the church, because the wording of this new law opened the door for female leadership on the parish level, and consequently created a new role for women in the Catholic church.

As in other complex organizations, the process of canon law revision involved a number of stages. Committees made up of bishops and canon lawyers (all males) spent many years analyzing the decrees of Vatican II, and then making the necessary changes in church law in order to bring the Code of Canon Law in line with the Vatican II documents. The earliest version of canon 517.2, published in 1977, was sent to the Catholic hierarchy and other consultative bodies of the church throughout the world in 1978. After observations of these groups were forwarded to the Vatican office, discussions on this proposed canon took place on April 19, 1980. As expected, some of the discussants in Rome "did not welcome the notion that a parish be entrusted, even in part," to a nonordained person.[18]

It was the intervention of Archbishop Rosalio Jose Castillo Lara from Venezuela that was the turning point in this deliberation.[19] He told the committee about the experience in his own diocese, where the priest shortage was particularly acute, and where the pastoral care of some communities was entrusted to nuns. Archbishop Castillo Lara expressed satisfaction with this arrangement, and he also argued that it was spiritually fruitful. This intervention by a Third World bishop was what finally convinced the committee, and the proposed canon was approved. If the earlier arguments of some of the committee members had prevailed, the inclusionary clause would have been deleted.

Thus, in 1983 when the new Code of Canon Law was promulgated, the door was opened for the appointment of women to a role that had previously been closed to them. Since canon 517.2 stipulates that a priest must be appointed to moderate the pastoral care provided by lay people, how radical a change is this, after all? Catholics who were parishioners before the decrees of Vatican II were promulgated can answer that, for they will remember that women were always seen but never heard in church, except as choir members. In fact, this author can recall being told by a priest in the early 1960s that it was a "mortal sin" for a woman to be present in the sanctuary (altar area) of the church during Mass. In the past twenty-five years, however, Catholic women had begun gradually to participate in parish roles which *required* their presence in the sanctuary during Mass, such as lectors (reading scripture), eucharist ministers (distributing communion), altar servers, and most recently, since the promulgation of canon 517.2, as administrators of priestless parishes.

The answer to the question, "Why Women Pastors?" is only partly answered by pointing to Vatican II changes and the revision of the Code of Canon Law. For a more complete answer to this question, we need to look at some external factors as well.

DEMOGRAPHIC CHANGES AND THE
CONTEMPORARY WOMEN'S MOVEMENT

Important demographic changes in the United States and the contemporary women's movement are the external factors that have expedited women's entrance into new roles in the church. Chief among the external demographic changes are women's greater participation in the labor force, their increased rate of college attendance, and their completion of postgraduate degrees.[20]

Concurrently, broad changes in external demographics are affecting the internal demographics of the Catholic church. The increasing shortage of priests is an example of these internal changes, and it is a key factor in the appointment of women to church positions that had previously been reserved solely for priests. Like the subject of the song, "Rosie the Riveter," written during the Second World War, women are being recruited to help out in a manpower shortage crisis. Appointing women as chancellors of dioceses, as canon lawyers in the diocesan tribunal, and as administrators of parishes can free priests for other diocesan needs, just as women working in factories freed male factory workers to fight in World War II.

The priest shortage is already in the crisis stage in some dioceses, as Schoenherr's national study indicates.[21] With regard to the situation in the United States, between 1966 and 1984 there was a twenty percent drop in the number of active diocesan priests, and it is predicted that between 1985 and the year 2005, there will be an additional twenty percent decline in the number of such priests available for active ministry. The most significant factor is recruitment: forty-six percent fewer priests were ordained between 1980 and 1984 than there were from 1966 to 1969. By the late 1990s the ordination rate will be sixty-nine percent lower than it was in the mid-sixties. Only six of every ten vacant positions are currently being filled by newly ordained priests.

The lower recruitment rate contributes to the rise in the average age of priests: forty-six percent of active diocesan clergy will be fifty-five years of age or over by the year 2005, and only twelve percent will be thirty-five or younger.[22] In contrast to the World War II manpower shortage, there is no anticipation of a future influx of male workers, because this shortage is due to retirements, resignations, and a steady decrease in recruitments over the past twenty-five years.

Were it not for the continued growth in Catholic membership in the United States, the situation would be less critical. The ratio of laity to priests over the past fifteen years has increased from 1,102 Catholics per priest in 1975 to a ratio of 1,418 in 1985, and Schoenherr predicts that there will be 2,193 laypersons per priest by 2005.[23] Since the priest shortage shows no sign of abating, and at the same time Catholic membership is steadily increasing, the recruitment of women to pastoring positions is not expected to be short-term.

The contemporary women's movement, which entered a phase of intense mobilization soon after the adjournment of the

Vatican Council, had important repercussions for Catholic women. It raised public consciousness regarding the second-class rank of women in the church. The gender caste system of the Catholic church, in which only men can attain the higher status of clergy while women—even those who join religious communities—are relegated to the ranks of the laity, was suddenly and starkly illuminated.

Have Catholics become more critical of the church's official position regarding the ordination of women? Greeley analyzed data from general social surveys at the National Opinion Research Center. Asked whether they thought "it would be a good thing if women were ordained as priests," American Catholics showed a fifteen percent increase in positive responses over an eight-year period. In 1974, twenty-nine percent agreed with the statement, but by 1982, forty-four percent agreed.[24] At present, slightly over half of Catholic adults no longer view the priesthood as a male prerogative, a twenty-three percent increase from 1974 to 1985.[25]

Some support for the ordination of women has come from professional groups within the church, such as the Catholic Biblical Association of America, which issued a report in 1979 concluding that the evidence in the New Testament, "while not decisive by itself, points toward the admission of women to priestly ministry."[26]

Individual members of the clergy have spoken out at various times in favor of women's ordination. For example, as early as 1970 sociologist Joseph Fichter, S.J. presented this challenge:

> What I am suggesting here is full equality of opportunity for women in the Catholic church. This means that women priests should be selected, appointed and promoted according to the same criteria employed for male priests. They should engage in both the parochial and special ministries of the church, receiving monsignorial honors if deserved, being appointed as chancery officials if competent, and reaching even the bishopric, cardinalate and papacy. Sex discrimination should go the way of ethnic and racial discrimination.[27]

In the early 1980s a few Catholic bishops in the United States wrote statements published in their dioceses addressing the problem of sexism in the church, and encouraged a rethinking of the role of women.[28] In 1990, the American bishops published the second draft of a pastoral letter[29] as a response to women's concerns. On the one hand the document condemned sexism as a sin, supported the theological preparation of women to preach the Gospel, recommended that "an incapacity to deal with women as equals should be considered a negative indication for fitness to ordination," and credited the women's movement for the part it played in helping nuns and laywomen to discover a new solidarity.

On the other hand, the document fell far short of the expectations of many Catholics. While admitting that there are "many women who can do what priests do," it sidestepped the issue of women's ordination by appealing to "unbroken tradition." It only went so far as to recommend that the question of women being ordained *as deacons* "be submitted to thorough investigation."[30]

The final vote on the proposed pastoral letter, which was to have been taken at the November 1990 national bishops' meeting, was postponed indefinitely on September 13, 1990. The explanatory statement by the committee making the decision cited as the principal reason "the need for more time and more consultation before the project reaches a conclusion." Another reason for the delay was that the Vatican had "suggested that consultation with bishops' conferences of other countries on this pastoral letter would be appropriate." Finally, it was argued that responses from the second draft of the proposed letter were still being received, and that the additional time would "allow a more reflective consideration of these responses."[31]

The women's movement was instrumental in other ways as well in regard to this movement of women into new roles in the church. Many American Catholic women experienced a heightening of their critical consciousness as they worked for the passage of the Equal Rights Amendment. These experiences helped some Catholic women to reflect on their countless hours of parish service and their exclusion from the most important functions in the ministry.

The use of gender-neutral language, an important agenda item of the contemporary women's movement, has gradually penetrated the Catholic church in the United States. For example, an excerpt from a consensus statement resulting from a symposium on Women and Church Law sponsored by the Canon Law Society of America in 1976 reads:

> We ask that the National Conference of Catholic Bishops, in conjunction with other Episcopal Conferences, work to replace sexist language in liturgical texts. We ask that such language be replaced in Conference statements, in existing Church legislation, and carefully avoided in any future statements and legislation.[32]

Some language revision in scripture readings, in hymns and prayers, and even in the revised Code of Canon Law has been accomplished, though much still remains to be done. The documents of Vatican II, some provisions in the new Code of Canon Law, demographic changes, and the contemporary women's movement have expedited the movement of women into new roles in the Catholic church. These facilitating factors help to explain why there are a few Catholic women serving as pastors of priestless parishes in the United States.

PREVIOUS AND CURRENT RESEARCH

One of the few previous studies of Catholic women pastors is Peter Gilmour's dissertation on priestless parishes, limited to nine rural parishes in the midwest: five in the west north central and four in the east north central regions of the United States. All of his parishes were predominantly white, and all were headed by nuns.[33] While he touches on some of the dilemmas experienced by the women administering these parishes, his book is predominantly descriptive of the context of the pastor's experience in each of these parishes. He focuses on this context in his interviews with the women pastors. Although there are a few statements from parishioners and priests in some of his chapters, it does not appear that he systematically interviewed parishioners and priests who were serving as sacramental ministers in each of the parishes.[34]

A national survey of administrators of priestless parishes in the United States that will be conducted under the auspices of the Institute for Pastoral Life is currently in the preparatory stage.[35] Located in Kansas City, Missouri, the Institute for Pastoral Life is a national center serving home mission dioceses characterized by vast geographic distances, sparse populations, and a poverty of resources. Established by a group of Catholic bishops in 1985, the institute focuses on the lay ministry needs of the parishes in these rural dioceses, and offers a direct training program of pastoral life coordinators (their title for laity heading priestless parishes) consisting of a three year cycle summer institute.

A perusal of the 1990 edition of the *Official Catholic Directory* revealed that there were 210 parishes in the United States administered by nonpriests. The largest portion of these parishes, sixty-one percent (129) were headed by nuns, twenty-two percent (47) were headed by deacons, nine percent (19) by laity, six percent (12) by religious brothers, and one percent (3) by pastoral teams.[36] Keeping in mind that the data for each edition of the *Directory* are gathered during the previous year, and the number of parishes headed by nonpriests increased from the previous edition (1989) by twenty-five, we can assume that at the present time there are approximately three hundred parishes or two percent of a total of 19,069 parishes in the United States being administered by nonpriests.[37] A recent edition of *Corpus Reports* cites a Vatican report that 157,000, or thirty-four percent of parishes worldwide, are without a priest; whereas in the United States ten percent of parishes are priestless.[38]

A research project on women appointed to administer parishes outside the United States was conducted by Katherine Gilfeather in Chile. Her study, entitled "The Changing Role of Women in the Catholic Church in Chile," was published in 1977. She reported that there were over eighty nuns acting as administrators of priestless parishes in many dioceses, doing tasks traditionally reserved for priests, and, as she said, "in general, taking the lion's share of responsibility for the spiritual welfare of the inhabitants."[39] As we know from the section in the earlier part of this chapter, these women were serving as pastors in spite of the fact that the new church law had not as yet been promulgated.

In 1987 I conducted an exploratory study of a small number of Catholic women who were in church positions that had been previously monopolized by men: chancellors of dioceses, canon lawyers, and administrators of priestless parishes.[40] The focus of that preliminary study, published in 1988, was on the creation of a new social reality for Catholic women; that is, on the causes rather than the consequences of recruitment to these new roles. Nonetheless, the data from those in-depth interviews shed some light on the consequences of women's movement into these new roles. For example, I found that there were considerable limitations to the power and control exercised by Catholic women administrators.

The results of a national survey of American Catholic laity also shed some light on the acceptance of women as pastors.[41] A majority (sixty-five percent) of the respondents said that Catholic laity (men *and* women) should have the right to be in charge of a parish when the priest is absent. A quarter (twenty-seven percent) said the laity should not have this right, and eight percent said they were not sure. There were no significant gender differences on this item. Thus, women who are placed in charge of priestless parishes can expect to find that about two-thirds of the parishioners approve of their appointment and about one-fourth disapprove.[42]

What the survey could not tell us was how parishioners translate these attitudes into behavior as they interact with a lay administrator appointed to head their parish, particularly when the layperson is a woman. Left unanswered were such questions as the following: Do her parishioners give a woman leader the same quality and quantity of support they gave the previous pastors? What are the types of behavior which show that parishioners affirm or reject her position as parish leader? What are her perceptions regarding the constraints and resources experienced in her everyday life in this new position?

MY RESEARCH

During the month of May 1989, I wrote letters to twenty women throughout the United States who had been appointed by their bishops to administer priestless parishes—and who had been doing so for at least a year—asking them to participate in my study. Most of the names and addresses of the women included in this study were obtained from the 1988 *Official Catholic Directory,* others came from women pastors whom I had interviewed in an exploratory study, and a few names came from other people knowledgeable about this phenomenon.[43]

In the letter I identified myself as a sociologist and a lifelong

Catholic who was embarking on a research project on women who had been appointed to pastoral leadership roles in parishes with no resident priest. I expressed the hope that the findings of my study would help to smooth the transition process for women who would be appointed to this role in the future.

My letter explained that I planned to visit twenty parishes throughout the country, where I would spend the weekend conducting interviews with the woman heading the parish, with the priest who provides sacramental ministry, and with two elected lay leaders of the parish (one male and one female).[44] I also said that I planned to participate in all of the liturgies and other parish activities taking place that weekend.[45]

When I phoned them a week later to schedule my proposed visit to their parishes, all twenty of the women said that they were willing to participate in the study. In spite of the fact that they were leading very busy lives, they were willing to contact the priest and parishioners and to arrange the time and place for my interviews prior to my arrival. When I asked them to recommend a hotel or motel nearby where I could make a reservation, most of them invited me to stay with them, either at the parish house or at their own homes. They also agreed to send me a copy of the history of the parish, where such a document existed, so that I could acquaint myself with the context of their situation before I arrived on the scene.

However, in making those initial phone calls, I discovered that two of the women had been recently terminated by their bishops, and a month later, I learned of a third termination. I substituted the next three names on my list for these three who were no longer living in their parishes; but I asked all three terminated women if they would agree to an interview, even though they would no longer be working in the same location. All three agreed, and I was able to conduct in-depth interviews with them as well.

One criterion for inclusion in the study was that these women appointed by the bishop as pastoral administrators had served in this capacity for at least one year. The total number of women who had been appointed to administer a parish before July 1, 1988, and whose names, addresses, and phone numbers were on my list, was eighty, so my sample represents one-fourth of the total population.

Initially I assumed that nuns would have an easier adjustment to the new role than laywomen, because parishioners
would perceive them as having a higher religious status as
exemplified by their vows, their title, and, in some cases, their
dress. Although nuns are not members of the clergy, and they
are, strictly speaking, laywomen, Catholics tend to place them in
a separate category, "a level above" the laity. Even though they
cannot be called "Father," religious women do have the title "Sister," which is not shared by their lay counterparts.

In order to compare the experiences of laywomen with that
of nuns, I chose nine parishes headed by laywomen and eleven
headed by nuns. To my knowledge, these nine laywomen were
the only women who had served as a pastor for a year or more,
and who were not members of religious communities. As mentioned earlier, sixty-one percent of nonpriest-headed parishes in
the United States are led by female members of religious communities. However, this proportion will change radically in the near
future because women's religious communities, like the priesthood, are experiencing a steady decrease in numbers of applicants.[46] Thus we can expect to see a continuing increase in the
numbers of laywomen appointed to head parishes. Therefore, I
overrepresented the number of laywomen in my sample, because
I considered their involvement to be the wave of the future, given
the increasing shortage of both priests and nuns.

Parishes headed by laywomen who were not nuns were
geographically dispersed in four of the nine census regions in
the United States. In order to include the eastern and southern
part of the United States, I included parishes headed by nuns in
two additional census regions. Although I traveled to twelve
states in all, I will not reveal the specific states in order to safe-
guard the anonymity of the people I interviewed.

The following are the six census regions represented in my
study and the number of parishes I visited in each: (1) Middle
Atlantic (New York, New Jersey, Pennsylvania), two parishes; (2)
East North Central (Wisconsin, Illinois, Indiana, Michigan, Ohio),
four parishes; (3) West North Central (Minnesota, Iowa, Missouri,
North Dakota, South Dakota, Nebraska, Kansas), three parishes;
(4) South Atlantic (Delaware, Maryland, West Virginia, Virginia,
North Carolina, South Carolina, Georgia, Florida, District of

Columbia), three parishes; (5) West South Central (Arkansas, Oklahoma, Louisiana, Texas), three parishes; and (6) Pacific (Washington, Oregon, California, Alaska, Hawaii), five parishes. In all, then, I traveled to twenty parishes representing fourteen dioceses and located in twelve states.

How "representative" was my sample? I combined the census regions into four categories and compared my sample to the total number of parishes headed by nonpriests in the United States (210) as reported in the 1990 *Official Catholic Directory*.[47] What I found was that in three of the regions my parishes were very similar: The largest cluster of nonpriest-headed parishes nationally is in the Midwest, forty percent (84), compared to thirty-five percent (7) of my parishes. The next largest cluster is in the South, thirty-two percent (68), compared to thirty percent (6) of my parishes. Another large cluster is in the West, twenty-six percent (55), compared to twenty-five percent (5) of my parishes. The region where I purposely oversampled, because I was aware that very few parishes were headed by nonpriests, was in the Northeast. Nationally only two percent (4) of the parishes in the Northeast are headed by nonpriests, compared to ten percent (2) of my parishes.

Another key assumption was that the climate of opinion created by supportive bishops would ease the transition into the new role for all women pastors. Thus I wanted to compare the experiences of women who were administering parishes located in dioceses headed by supportive bishops with those whose bishops were either neutral or nonsupportive. Bishops who engaged in activities such as the following were considered supportive: writing a public statement in support of women's greater participation in the church; visiting the parish prior to the appointment to explain to the parishioners the reasons for her appointment; making a public announcement of the appointment in the diocesan newspaper; participating in her formal installation ceremony in the parish; and including her in all the official mailings sent to other (male) pastors. Based on these criteria, half of the parishes in my sample are located in dioceses with supportive bishops.

I was also interested in rural-urban differences. My assumption was that Catholics living in large cities where there are many churches could simply attend Mass at another church if they did not approve of a woman as pastor. Likewise, Catholics living in smaller communities would have fewer alternatives for Sunday worship services, and would be more inclined to cooperate in order to keep their parish open. I wanted to compare the experiences of women whose parishes were located in large cities with those located in smaller communities. However, I soon found that the great majority of parishes headed by women were located in small rural communities, so only two large city parishes could be included.

When I visited these parishes between June and December 1989, I stayed for the weekend, usually three days and two nights, and in most cases I was their guest in the rectory or parish house. I conducted taped interviews not only with the woman in charge of the parish, but also with the priest who came to celebrate Mass and administer the sacraments (often called the sacramental minister), and two parishioners, one male and one female, who were members of the parish council.[48] I describe these interviews as in-depth because I spent approximately two hours interviewing each pastor, and one hour each with the priest and two parishioners. The interviews were also semistructured because, although there were specific open-ended questions asked, I also probed wherever feasible, and gave the interviewee many opportunities for input that was not included in the interview schedule.[49]

In addition to four interviews at each parish, I also conducted taped interviews with the three women who had been terminated as pastors shortly after they had agreed to participate in the study. The total number of in-depth interviews, therefore, was eighty-three.

While visiting at the parishes I would often hold informal interviews with parishioners, that I recorded in my field notes. I also gathered data by observing the interaction between the woman who was pastoring the parish and her central role partners (priest and parishioners) at the various parish functions occurring over the weekend, such as the worship services where she and/or the priest are the presiders, and other church activities, like baptisms, weddings, visits to the sick, coffee and donut gatherings after Mass, church dinners, and meetings of the parish council. Since in most cases I was a guest in their homes, and often traveled with the women pastors to church functions, I was able to observe them in their daily lives and to discuss a variety of topics with them.

With the cooperation of the woman pastor, I was also able to collect some documentary data such as parish histories, church bulletins, diocesan guidelines regarding lay pastors, contracts, letters of appointment, and relevant local newspaper articles. The data for this book, then, include the tape-recorded interviews, the informal conversations and observations that I recorded in a notebook during my visit to the parish, and documents.

The Lilly Endowment grant enabled me to hire a professional person for the next stage of the research project, the transcription of the interview tapes that were stored on disks as well as printed out. The database also included participant observation field notes and documentary material that were likewise stored on disks. After completing the coding of the data, I was aided in the data-retrieval stage by a graduate student research assistant, provided for by the National Science Foundation grant. Data were retrieved and analyzed by using a variant of Word Perfect's search and retrieve functions. When this was completed I was then able to begin the final write-up stage of the project.

The title of this book is *They Call Her Pastor*. Although the title "pastor" is, strictly speaking, reserved for priest-pastors,[50] I soon found that not only were these women doing the work of priest-pastors, but they were often referred to as the pastor. For instance, at least three of their bishops introduced them as pastor in public, and the mail they received from the diocesan administration offices often addressed them as pastor. Most of the parishioners I interviewed said they considered their woman administrator to be their pastor, and referred to her as pastor when speaking of her to people outside the parish.

Several of the priests who were serving as sacramental ministers for the parish also called them pastor. One of the priests put it this way,

> The sense that I got right away is that she is in many ways the pastor of the parish. I remember telling other people this. If there is a problem, they always go to a pastor. So I guess I knew right away that she really was the leader of the parish.

•2•

A Portrait of the Pastors and Their Parishes

This chapter is an attempt to present a picture of the women pastors in this study and their parishes. In filling out the portrait we look first at who the women are, in terms of some of their background characteristics. Then the question, "Where do they come from?" is answered by looking at how they were recruited to their present positions. Finally, we look at some of their personal characteristics as seen by them, by their parishioners, and by their sacramental ministers.

WHO ARE THEY?

What do these women pastors look like? Their ages range from thirty-three to sixty-seven, averaging fifty years of age. In general their ages help them to blend in quite well with their parishioners, even the women at the extremes of the age range. For example, the youngest was appointed to a rural parish of predominantly young families, and she and her young family fit right in. The oldest woman pastor told me that she thought her grey hair was an advantage in her dealings with the priests of the diocese. She is convinced that they would not have accepted her as readily, nor would she have been taken as seriously by them, had she been a younger woman. Seventeen of the woman pastors are white, and three are Mexican-American.[1]

Eleven of the parishes were headed by nuns, eight by married women, and one by a single laywoman.[2] All of the married women had children, from a low of three to a high of six, with an average of 3.5 children. However, only five of the married women had children who were still living at home with them. The husbands of the married women had full-time jobs with the exception of one who was retired. All of the husbands were living at home, though two of them had jobs requiring considerable out-of-town travel.

In general, all of the women pastors are college educated women. Although not all of them have college degrees, they had some college experience. Seven had one to three years of college, and thirteen have bachelor's degrees. Of the thirteen with bachelor's degrees, twelve have graduate degrees as well: three have two master's degrees, eight have one master's degree, and one was currently a master's candidate. In order to keep abreast in the field of parish ministry, several of the women were taking courses in theology at nearby colleges, attending workshops and seminars, and participating in in-service training conferences. When we discussed their preparation for church services, it was evident that they also made a serious attempt to keep up with their reading.

Some of these women have achieved a higher level of education than their sacramental ministers, although many of the women draw on the greater pastoral experience of the priests.

During an interview with a priest who had never received a bachelor's degree, he proudly described his role in the in-service training of the woman pastor with a master's degree:

> So I really was available to train her. I wish now, looking back, that she had enrolled in a couple of different kinds of programs that would have given her a little bit of experience with something like canon law. She had no idea what dispensations were for marriages, why you might need a dispensation for one thing and a permission for another, how you set up sponsors for baptisms, and what you require of people and what you do for marriage preparation.

He continued:

> I had to get books for her and I had to explain to her what our policies were here, though I did not impose those policies upon her. I tried to explain to her, one by one, when situa-

tions arose what to do. "What do I do with this bill that came in from the chancery?" It took a lot of time. I was on call for the first year, and then it still continues where now (she) prepares a yellow pad of questions and things she wants to talk about and then she'll say, "Can I get together with you?" And we'll just go through the whole number of things and she'll ask about them.

The education differential becomes more apparent when the preaching styles of priest and woman pastor are compared. I heard the women preach in eleven of the parishes I visited.[3] In five of the nine parishes where I was unable to hear the woman preach, it was the priest's "turn" that weekend. In the remaining four parishes, the woman pastor only preached rarely and/or on special occasions.

With respect to the preaching that I did observe, my impression was that these women not only prepared their sermons very carefully, but they also delivered them well, and tended to make a connection between the scripture reading and the daily lives of their parishioners. Some of the women pastors were very creative in the way they asked questions of the congregation while they were preaching. For example, when one of them asked, "Who would rather die than sin?" in the middle of her presentation, you could have heard a pin drop in the church.

Because they cared deeply about communicating effectively with their parishioners in their homilies, preparation time was a priority for these pastors. As one of them explained, "I don't think I would want to preach every week. I wouldn't mind every other week because I prepare, and I don't think I would have time."

One of the priests, well liked by the parishioners, delivered a weak and somewhat disconnected homily[4] during the Mass I attended. The woman pastor, who had a good sense of how to touch the parishioners, gave him an article as we were drinking coffee after Mass, about the scripture readings for a future Sunday, and he was most grateful for it. He explained that she often shared valuable preaching material with him.

One of the sacramental ministers, whose education was equal to or greater than the pastor's, praised her creativity in this way:

I think she is more creative and more personally attentive to things, whereas I might accept doing something just because that's the way it's always been done, or doing something because that's how the book explained it should be done right then or take the easy way out that way. I don't think she does that very often. I think she really sits down and thinks, "What is this?" and how it should be done and "What's the reason for it?" and "How should I go about it." At least I see some of that.

An example would be the commentary at Mass. I just take a commentary that's canned, and I will clean it up a little if it needs it. It is one that somebody else does and I take it. I think she does her own always. I am sure she may use some other sources on occasion, but I am sure she puts more energy into that than I do.

On the other hand, one of the woman pastors, with less education than her sacramental minister, only rarely preached, even though urged to do so by priests and parishioners. She described herself this way:

> I am an introvert and he [the previous pastor] was a one hundred percent extrovert, very outgoing and expansive. For me, it isn't a natural thing to get up and do some of the things I am now doing, so in that way I have to work at it harder.
>
> The real problem...for me is the preparation time. But both of them [sacramental ministers] give excellent homilies and so I am nervous about getting up and giving it, but I do it.

With regard to previous work experience, there is a range among the women pastors, varying from teaching to sales and clerical work. When asked about previous full-time occupations, fifteen women mentioned more than one; twelve listed two previous full-time jobs and three of them mentioned three occupations. Fourteen of the women mention teaching as an earlier full-time occupation; ten of the fourteen former teachers are members of religious communities. All of the former teachers viewed their previous experience as a good preparation for the job of pastor. One of them, who had been a primary school teacher, explained:

> I think I have an intuition about people because I had to when I was in a classroom with little kids in the very beginning stages of learning. I don't mean that as a putdown at all, I just mean that I don't take some things for granted. It is something where you have to explain things clearly, and don't make

assumptions that people know what you are talking about, using phrases and words that assume they know. They don't always. Church jargon is a jargon, and sometimes it isn't understood. It's a whole different language sometimes. And because so much of what I do is teaching, I am grateful for the skills of group process and dynamics that I have developed.

Another former teacher told me that she writes her sermons almost a week ahead of schedule because the unexpected (like funerals) can always happen. She said she felt that her twenty-two years as a teacher making lesson plans for her classes were a good preparation.

Two of the women had previous experience as a pastor; this is their second parish. Seven of them list "pastoral associate" as a former full-time occupation; seven of them had experience in managerial or administrative positions; five are former directors of religious education; and three mentioned sales and clerical as previous occupations. All of them had worked primarily in the United States, but four of the eleven nuns had spent some time working in Third World countries as well. Table 1 summarizes the pastors' characteristics.

WHERE DO THEY COME FROM?

Half of the women could be described as "outsiders," meaning that when they were appointed to the parish, they were recruited from another city or town. Only four of the ten outsiders were recruited from outside the diocese, and those four were members of religious communities. One was asked by the diocesan personnel director to apply for the job; another belonged to a religious community that had asked the bishop to appoint a member to head the parish. In the third case, the sister was recruited from outside the diocese through a priest who had had a positive experience with a sister who had served under him as a pastoral associate in charge of religious education. As he described it,

> About twelve years ago, at another parish where I was, I approached the...Sisters and asked them if they had someone who would want to come and share a ministry in a parish. Then they contacted me and told me that someone was available and a few people came up for interviews, and we hired

Table 1
Characteristics of Women Pastors

	Age*	Education	Occupations**	Married
1.	Middle	Some College	Teacher/Sales	Yes
2.	Younger	Some College	Teacher/Mgr.	Yes
3.	Older	M.A.	Teacher/PA	No
4.	Middle	M.A.	PA	No
5.	Older	Some College	Mgr./PA	No
6.	Younger	B.A.	Mgr./PA	Yes
7.	Middle	M.A.	Teacher/DRE	No
8.	Younger	M.A.	Teacher/DRE/Mgr.	No
9.	Middle	Some College	Teacher/Mgr.	Yes
10.	Middle	M.A.	Teacher/DRE/PA	No
11.	Middle	M.A.	Teacher	No
12.	Younger	B.A.	Teacher/DRE	Yes
13.	Middle	M.A.	Teacher/Mgr.	No
14.	Middle	M.A.	Teacher/PA	No
15.	Middle	Some College	Sales/Clerical	Yes
16.	Middle	M.A.	Teacher/PA	No
17.	Older	Some College	Mgr.	Yes
18.	Younger	Some College	Clerical	Yes
19.	Older	M.A.	Teacher/DRE/PA	No
20.	Middle	M.A.	Teacher/PA	No

*Age categories: Younger (Under 46), Middle (46–55), Older (56+).
**Previous Full-Time Occupations: PA denotes either pastoral associate or pastoral administrator; DRE denotes director of religious education; Mgr. denotes managerial/administrative positions.

one as a pastoral associate. At that time I didn't bother to check through the diocese. We just hired [her] and then I informed the diocese that there was a sister working in the parish and there was no problem with that at all. And then it became a very acceptable situation when we found out just how well we were working together.

This strategy, hiring a woman as a pastoral associate to be in charge of a specific program—such as religious education or liturgy—and to work with the resident priest, has been used by some priest pastors as a "first step" toward the recruitment of women pastors. In a sense this is a form of in-service training for the women, and it is especially helpful in dioceses headed by bishops who are reluctant to appoint nonpriests as pastors, where there is no training program available.

This same priest quoted above became alarmed when he was appointed as pastor to a large parish where the neighboring pastor who administered two additional parishes was due to retire. Realizing that he might soon be asked to take over the duties at the neighboring parish, he contacted the sister in charge of religious women in his diocese and told her that he would like a sister to come up and administer these parishes. Because he succeeded in convincing the bishop of the need for alternate staffing, he was able to recruit a sister as pastoral administrator.

The fourth "outsider" sister who came from another diocese to be in charge of a parish took the initiative herself by asking the bishop to appoint her:

> I called [the bishop] up and said to him, "I am thinking of changing my job, and I wonder if there is anything in your diocese." And he said, as he always does, "Well, let's talk about it." So I had an appointment in January and I went up to [his diocese] and he said to me, "Well, what do you really want to do?" And when he said that, it freed me up to muse with him about it. But I never really said I wanted to be in charge of a parish until, as we talked, that is what it was leading to. And he listened. And then he began to talk about the shortage of priests.

She continued:

> It wasn't that long a visit, about forty-five minutes. After that, I said to him, "Would you ever consider me?" And he said, "Yes." He said, "I will be in touch with you within a couple of weeks." And within a couple of weeks I heard from him, and he said, "I am putting this in the hands of [the sister who was Personnel Director for the diocese]. I want her to negotiate how this will all work, and I have two places I have in mind, and I want to see how you feel, and we will work it out."

This bishop quoted above is very supportive of the idea of laity running parishes. In fact, his view is that ordination does not always produce good pastors, and he tries to place his priests in positions where they can utilize their strengths. So he appointed someone from outside the diocese with the gifts for pastoring, rather than closing the parish, or appointing an unsuitable priest.

ENTERING THE PARISH

Outsiders tended to experience more difficulty as they moved into the new role of pastor than did insiders. One of them described what she saw and did when she arrived at the parish house:

> The first week I moved into this house it was filthy dirty because no one took care of it. I came in and this house was overrun with mice, and dirty. I just started cleaning. And the people watched, and nobody came over and said, "Can I help?" They all knew what I was doing. This whole village knew what I was doing, but they were so nervous and so unsure of who I was or what I was doing here that they didn't approach me.

In fact it took most of the outsiders an entire year before they felt that they were accepted by the parishioners. The first few weeks were especially painful, as one of the outsiders attests:

> In the beginning I knew that if I didn't get out, I would just be sitting all by myself in here [the parish house] and I would never meet anybody because they certainly were not going to come to me. They were not going to come up and say, "Welcome!" I had to walk out or else I would die here. So I would just walk around town and meet people on the streets. Then, of course, they talked to each other. It's such a small town that everybody knows everything. And the same way at church, I would make sure I talked to every single person as much as I could. But it was real important; otherwise I would never get into their lives because they would not include me or invite me.

An outsider who described her parishioners as shy and low on self-esteem said,

> They are hard to get real close to because they don't communicate in terms of telling you how they feel. They have told me that unless you are born here, you will always be an outsider.

A parishioner described a confrontation that took place between an "outsider" woman pastor and another parishioner soon after the woman pastor's arrival at the parish. One of the parishioners who came to the parish house took it upon herself to inform the pastor that "the people do not want you here and (they) want you to leave." The woman pastor responded by explaining that she had been assigned to the parish by the bishop, that it was he who had invited her. Clearly this kind of confrontation could have been avoided or at least alleviated if the bishop had involved the parishioners in the recruitment of the pastor.

One of the four women recruited from outside the diocese— and had been serving as the pastor for four years by the time I visited her—made this observation about coming from a city in another diocese to her rural parish:

> The framework of social life revolved in circles here. I had never lived in a rural area. I didn't expect that I wouldn't be included in social things because in every parish I've been in I had always been part of the social fabric of people's lives— invited to parties. I always was. And here I'm not, even now.

She continued,

> I don't even get invited to all the weddings that I slave over. I don't get invited to the receptions. Some I do, but not all. I don't get invited to parties after baptisms. I think it isn't that they are rejecting me. I think they are just so used to their groupings being family that it doesn't occur to them to extend invitations to outsiders.

Perhaps the fact that these outsiders were also members of religious communities was a partial reason for the lack of invitations. Although I had predicted that nuns would have an easier adjustment to this new role because of their perceived higher religious status, this was not always true, especially for those who were outsiders in the sense that they had not previously worked or lived in the parish. One of the parishioners explained her community's reaction to the appointment of an outsider nun as their pastor:

> In the beginning it was like, "Oh my God, a nun is going to start ruling, and things are going to be so strict." It's been so lax with the priests, because they haven't been here to enforce or meet the needs. Even fifty percent of the time they're not here; they're doing a job somewhere else. So the idea that someone was going to come here with new ideas and new

rules who was from a city—that created a problem also—the fact that she was not a rural person. A city person tends to have different ideas and run a faster pace than we're used to. We're a laid-back, rural community.

One of the outsider nuns described the parishioners' resistance to her appointment this way:

It was like, "This is our place; you are the outsider. You aren't like Father So-and-so; we have always done it this way."

Another woman coming from outside the diocese described the way she attempted to move toward becoming more of an insider, and compared herself to the previous resident pastor.

They [the parishioners] just stared straight past me. They were shy. They didn't know what I was doing here. It was not clearly explained to everybody. They didn't know what I would be doing, and they didn't know how to reach out to me. They are very, very family-oriented people. They are not like a city or suburban parish where everybody is a stranger to each other, so you are forced to relate to each other. They are very groupy. So, as they stood outside on the steps after Mass, I had to go and insert myself into their groups. Otherwise, they just ignored me. Now that's different, of course, but in the beginning that's how it was.

She then compared herself to the previous pastor:

I am doing it differently. I think that the deacon ahead of me had good administrative skills, but he was not a pastoral person. He didn't have that charisma. I have a good combination of both, so I am doing it differently. I am more outgoing than he was. I open the [parish] house; he never opened the house, letting people come in and have meetings in the living room. Generally, there is a different atmosphere.

A male parishioner from this same parish corroborated her analysis when he praised her for the way she had reached out to all members of the community for the past four years. As a consequence, he said,

We have a community spirit here. She has her finger on the pulse of the parish much more so than the deacon or the former priests.

One of the "outsider" women pastors used the strategy of involving the parishioners in more of the parish decision making, and thus making them more like "insiders." She explained,

> It's important to bring people into the planning, and on a much bigger level, of course, it's critical. They will never feel that it's their own parish if an outsider like me comes in and does what I want. It has to be done with the people. So we have committees and commissions. We move any kind of project into those commissions.

An outsider who was a member of a pastoral team and had just completed her first year in the parish had this to say about the acceptance of sisters as opposed to priests on the part of older parishioners.

> Father is very taken care of and he won't go hungry and he will always be invited to dinner. We are not invited to dinner. Some of our close friends and the younger families are real good. "Sister, come on over," and they are real informal. But the older ones, the staid relationships in the parish that have been here for years, that have always had Father at their dinner table, they don't have Sister at their dinner tables.

RECRUITMENT ROUTES

Although I had assumed that most of the women I would be visiting were recruited initially by their bishops, this was not the case for the four mentioned above who came from outside the diocese. I soon discovered that there was a variation in recruitment. The variations could be a function of the lack of planning in some dioceses, where the shortage of priests either took the bishop by surprise, or he had hoped to find other solutions, like recruiting priests from foreign countries. Even today there are many dioceses where no guidelines regarding training or recruitment to these positions exist. These tend to be dioceses with an adequate supply of priests, where the bishop has not addressed future shortages.

On the other hand, some dioceses have recently turned to national advertising. For example:

The Archdiocese of Anchorage is recruiting for pastoral administrators in rural parishes. Qualifications: M.A. in divinity or
theology or equivalent and experience in parish ministry. Must
be willing to live in a rural setting that calls for flexibility. Send
resume to: Director of Pastoral Services and Ministries, Archdiocese of Anchorage, 225 Cordova St., Anchorage, AK 99501.[5]

As more and more dioceses turn to national advertising, we
can expect to find an increase in the number of lay pastors who
are recruited from outside the diocese. Advertising in the local
diocesan paper would probably be the first choice for most bishops, who would consider someone from the diocese as less an
"outsider." In fact, it was extremely successful in one parish I
visited, where there had been fifty applicants for the position
advertised in their diocesan newspaper.

There was a variety of "paths" to the door of the parish house
for the women pastors interviewed. Although all of the women
were appointed by the bishop, in seven of the cases a priest
(either a local pastor or the diocesan personnel director) recruited
her, as in one of the examples above. One of the priests, aware
that his term of appointment at the parish was in the final year,
recruited a sister as pastoral associate and after training her for
the job, convinced the bishop to appoint her to head the parish
after his departure. One of the sisters who was recruited as part of
a team by the diocesan personnel director said,

> We have begun to establish a trust level here. Father _____ is
> convinced that if people have a good experience of liturgy,
> and have good, solid homilies, and you are there for them in
> their grief, that they will come, no matter who you are. And
> that has certainly proved true. We have listened to them, we
> have identified their pain [regarding the loss of a resident
> priest pastor]; we have given them permission to be angry.
> And then we have buried them, married them, blessed them,
> prayed with them, cried with them. So, therefore, when we go
> to them and say, "Would you help us?" nobody turns us down.

In five cases the parishioners chose the woman to be the
pastoral administrator, and recommended her to the bishop. All
five of these were insiders, meaning that they had lived or
worked in the parish prior to their appointment. Three were laywomen who had been active members of the parish for many

years, and two were nuns who, at the time of the appointment, had been serving as pastoral associates in the parish for more than four years. The general scenario for the recruitment of these five insiders was similar. Typically, the bishop met with the parish council to explain that he had no priest to replace the one who was leaving or retiring. He explained that they could close the parish, recruit a foreign priest, advertise the position in the diocese or nationally, or appoint one of the members of the parish. After weighing the alternatives, the parishioners said, "We want her!" and the bishop complied with their choice.

In four cases it was the woman herself who was the initiator; two of them applied for the position that was advertised, and two asked the bishop to consider them for appointment to a parish which had recently lost its pastor, but where no decision about the successor had been made. One of the outsiders who took this latter path to the parish house described her experience earlier in this chapter. The other unique path to the door of the parish house was taken by a married woman who was aware that a neighboring parish had recently lost its resident pastor. Apparently no steps towards the recruitment of a replacement had been taken. She, however, could be considered an insider, because she had previously been a member of this parish, and knew many of the parishioners very well. Her strategy was to write a letter to the bishop, which she shared with me. The following are excerpts from her letter:

> Dear Bishop _____ :
>
> It is my understanding that the [parish] is still without a pastor at this time. I would like to ask that you consider appointing me as a [pastoral administrator]. I feel that my background in the church has given me the skills that would be valuable in this ministry.

After enumerating her training in pastoral ministry and her years of experience in working for the church in many capacities, she continued,

> Although we are registered at [her own parish], we live in the boundaries of [the parish without a pastor], and I am well acquainted with the needs of that parish. There are many challenges in serving that parish due to its essentially rural nature

and ethnic composition. The...area in the past has demonstrat-
ed its openness to fresh approaches to the presence of the
church among its people, and I feel would be receptive to the
appointment of a [pastoral administrator] to serve the...area.
    Thank you for your consideration.

The bishop in question referred her application to the members of the diocesan personnel board, who recommended that
she be appointed to the position. Before her appointment, however, the bishop asked her to consult with the parish council to
see if they would support the appointment. She felt this was a
good move on the part of the bishop because, as she explained,
"If they don't support me, I would not be able to function effectively in the first six months anyway." However, she also realized
that the bishop's condition of prior consultation with the parishioners might have some long range effects. She continued,

> However, he may not know that he is setting a precedent that
> may come back and haunt him when he gets ready to assign a
> priest somewhere and a strong parish council says, "We want
> to be consulted." I did not point that out to him, because I
> didn't think about it at the time.

In most of the parishes I visited, the process included consultation with the parishioners before the appointment was made.
One of the women pastors who had been interviewed by the
parishioners before her appointment, explained why she considered herself a good "fit" for her rural parish in a small town.

> I was really interested in getting involved in total parish activi-
> ty. I felt this kind of parish would give me that possibility. It
> was very similar to my hometown situation, and I felt I could
> identify with that. I felt I could relate to the people in a town
> like this.

There were, however, three cases where prior consultation
would have smoothed the process considerably for women who
were outsiders. Because these women were "foisted on them"
by the bishop without any parishioner input, the parishioners
were understandably upset, and put themselves at a distance
from their woman pastor. Needless to say, these three women
pastors did not see any welcome signs when they arrived at the
parish; in fact they felt that they were ignored by most parish-

ioners in the first weeks of their ministry. One of the parishioners said that there was only a small group who accepted her as pastor at the very beginning. As she explained,

> I think she felt a cold shoulder from the majority of the people here, and that was very, very hard for her. And I know that she presented herself a little more gruffly to people because she didn't feel accepted. And her front was to buckle up and be very stern, and that came across like, "Oh boy, is she ever a strict nun." Their strict-nun image was really there anyway for a lot of people.

One of these three also had multiple stresses during her first year as pastor, and she told me that she cried herself to sleep on more than one occasion that first year. She was described by a female parishioner in this way:

> She's a very tough lady. She puts up a very strong front and then when she accepts the situation for what it is, she kind of goes forward and attacks that situation and tries to break it down. And she's very good. I've seen her go up to people who are not accepting of her and give them a hug. And it's hard to resist somebody who's giving you a hug, somebody who's sharing themselves with you that way. And I've seen her break through on a lot of people. Sometimes it just takes time; sometimes they're just not ready to accept her and she just needs to leave it go. But if she sees that they are a receptive person at all, then she is very quick to go forward and try to break the ice herself. And it takes a lot of energy, a lot of emotion to do that.

What were the recruitment routes of the four remaining outsiders whom I visited? In three cases it was the bishop who initiated the recruitment of the woman pastor, and in one case it was the head of the woman's religious community who asked her to consider accepting the position, once the community convinced the bishop to appoint one of their members.

The other half of the women pastors were insiders. One of them had lived in the parish all her life, and another had only worked in the parish for a year before her appointment, but the median amount of time spent in the parish prior to the appointment by these insiders was six years. The ten insiders had a distinct advantage as they moved into their new role as pastor, in that they were already known, respected, and loved by many of the parishioners. In addition, their parishioners feared for the survival of the parish. As one of them told me,

> I think we were all leery because of the new situation. We had always had a priest being our administrator. Right from the time I started going to church here, we felt our church continuing was a precarious situation because we were small, and there were many larger parishes in need of priests. And we were really told that our doors may be closed if it came to the point where we couldn't afford to keep ourselves open to have a priest available to us. So when we heard that we were not going to be a parish that had a full-time priest anymore, we were all very shaken for fear that the church may cease to be.

THE CONTEXT OF THEIR PARISHES

As described earlier, the women pastors are located in twenty parishes dispersed in twelve states in six of the nine census regions in the United States. Thirty-five percent (7) of the parishes are in the Midwest (East and West North Central regions); thirty percent (6) in the South (South Atlantic, East and West South Central regions); twenty-five percent (5) in the West (Mountain and Pacific regions); and ten percent (2) are in the Northeast (Middle Atlantic region). All but two of the parishes are located in small towns or villages in rural areas that are not identified in order to protect the anonymity of interviewees.

The eastern part of the United States, and in particular New England, is not well represented in this study, although two of the women pastors are located in the Middle Atlantic region. Unfortunately, it was impossible to select any parishes in the New England region, which includes Maine, Vermont, New Hampshire, Massachusetts, Connecticut, and Rhode Island, because there were no women appointed in any of these states as pastoral administrators with the requisite experience when the research was planned.

Initially, I expected to find each woman in charge of one parish where a priest, appointed as the sacramental minister, appeared each weekend to celebrate Mass and preside at the sacraments. I soon discovered that there were many "atypical" situations.

First of all, there were only twelve parishes where the woman pastor was administering only one parish, and the appointed sacramental minister arrived every weekend to celebrate Mass. Secondly, there were three parishes where the interview with the pastor involved two people. In one case I held a joint interview with a married couple who were copastoring in a parish, and in two cases I held joint interviews with two nuns who were part of a diocesan team serving four parishes. The other members of the team were the priests, and in one case, a deacon also, all of whom took turns presiding at either Mass or communion services in the parishes they served.

However, even in some of these "typical" parishes, the responsibility for providing a sacramental minister was often placed in the hands of the woman pastor when the appointed sacramental minister was on vacation or had responsibilities elsewhere.

In four of the "atypical" parishes, there was a Mass every weekend, but the same priest did not appear each time. Two of the women pastors had two priests who rotated as sacramental ministers every weekend, one woman pastor had three rotating priests, and one had four different priests per month. In the latter case, both pastor and parishioners mentioned that they enjoyed having different preachers each week, even though much of the pastor's time had to be spent in contacting and scheduling the priests' visits. The fact that these priests had other full-time jobs made rotation necessary. For instance, one of the priests assigned as the sacramental minister for one of the parishes was also the vocation director for the diocese. He explained his limitations thus:

> I don't go out there [to her parish as sacramental minister] every weekend. As vocation director, I have to keep two weekends a month available when I go out to fill in for priests, or go to their parishes to speak on vocations during weekend Masses. And then the two or three weekends that I am here I fill in. When I am gone, [she] has to find another priest in the area who is available, or she has to hold a communion service.

In the remaining four "atypical" parishes the priest did not appear every weekend, usually because he was serving two or three other parishes in addition to his own, and/or because the driving distances were so immense. Three of the parishes had Mass every other weekend; in one of these it was the same priest who appeared, but in two others there were two different priests who appeared on alternate weeks. Finally, in the most atypical case, the parishioners in one parish sometimes saw a priest only once a month. The woman pastor explained,

> He [the bishop] promised to send a priest twice a month and that was not fulfilled. In the beginning, yes, but after awhile whoever was available would come and sometimes three Sundays in a row we wouldn't have anybody. In the beginning [of her term as administrator] I would call him and remind him, and there came a moment in which I thought that he is the bishop and he is the one who has the responsibility. If we have several Sundays without a priest, it is his responsibility. We are doing the best we can. Now, again, we are having this priest twice a month. For awhile we went three or four weeks without one.

In those eight parishes where the priest does not appear each weekend, the woman pastor presides at a word and communion service. This service consists of introductory prayers, readings from the scriptures, a reflection on the scripture readings (sermon), and the distribution of communion. The hosts used for this service were previously consecrated by a priest during Mass, and preserved for this purpose. I was able to observe four of the women pastors presiding at these services.

Most of the women (15) were in charge of only one parish, four administered in two parishes, and one was in charge of a parish and two missions. How many parishioners were these women responsible for? Most parishes count members by families or households, but "family" was the term that was used most often. The range in number of families in the twenty parishes was from 339 to 50. There were five "large" parishes (200–400 families), ten "medium-size" parishes (100–199 families), and five "small" parishes (under 100 families).[6] The median number of families for whom the women pastors were responsible was 147, which is roughly three hundred-fifty parishioners.

With respect to racial or ethnic characteristics, fifteen of the parishes could be described as predominantly white. The two that were predominantly Mexican-American were situated in the South and in the West. There was one black parish located in the South. In addition, there was one in the South that was almost equally black and white, and another in the West that had an equal portion of white and Mexican-American parishioners. Most of the white women pastors were heading predominantly white parishes, though one was pastoring a mixed black and white parish and another a predominantly Mexican-American parish. One of the Mexican-American women pastors headed a predominantly Mexican-American parish; one headed a black parish; and the third was a member of a pastoral team serving a parish that had an equal mix of Mexican-American and white parishioners.

Ten of the women live in a rectory, usually situated next to the church. Most of them refer to it as the parish house, because by definition a rectory is the residence of a parish priest. Half of the women living in the parish house live with someone else, either a member of their religious community, or in the case of one young married woman, with husband and children. The remaining five live in the parish house alone and are ambivalent about their living situations. One of them told me that she doesn't mind living alone because she is so busy throughout the day, and gone so much, that she appreciates the quiet and space when she returns home. Ideally, however, she would like to have someone to share with, to pray with, to "do things" with. However, she said she would prefer to live alone rather than have someone thrust on her, someone she hadn't chosen as a living companion. At least two of the others are "loners" and their attitudes about their present living situation is very positive.

Seven of the eight married women live in their own homes situated within the parish boundaries. Two of these married women have converted a room in their home to an office, because the church has not yet been built. The three remaining women pastors are living in rented homes near the church.

There was no church building in three of the twenty parishes I visited, although building plans are in progress in two of these parishes. In one case the land for the church had already been donated, and the building campaign was underway. When the woman pastor showed me the site for the church, she estimated that the building would be completed within a year or two. In the second parish, the building plans were limping along, and the parishioners were skeptical about the outcome.

Church services are held in nearby Protestant churches in two of the three parishes without their own building. In one case the Mass is celebrated on Saturday evening, a time when it is not needed by the host congregation. In the other case the Mass is celebrated early on Sunday morning, just before the Protestant service. In the third parish, Mass is held in the auditorium of a public school building on Sunday morning. These situations present constraints for all three of the women pastors. Problems include lack of adequate storage space, of classroom space for religious education, and of a meeting place for committees and social gatherings. Two of the women pastors have converted space in their own homes to be used as a temporary parish office, and one of them uses a rented office near the church. Needless to say, these women and their parishioners are looking forward to the day when their church buildings are completed. One of the male parishioners located in the parish where Mass was said in a public school building said,

> Speaking of funerals, one of the things that's been real difficult is that we don't have a church, so we have to make arrangements with other parishes in order to have a funeral service. [The woman pastor] has to do that.

The yearly salary of these women ranged from $3000 to $25,300. The two women with the lowest salaries did not work full-time, so if we subtract their wages in order to calculate the average full-time salaries, the average salary is $12,000. What we should keep in mind is that the salary is paid by the parish, which in this study was typically located in a poor and isolated area. Understandably, then, the women pastors cannot expect higher salaries, even though their education and experience dictates that they should.

Half of these women lived in the parish house rent-free, so their actual remuneration was higher. When I calculated the free housing as an additional salary of $500 monthly for those who lived in the parish house, then the average full-time salary comes to $15,500. Although the contracts varied, other monies were also usually allocated for medical and health insurance, gas for the car when used for parish business, and continuing education courses or workshops. Also typically provided were one day off per week, a week for spiritual retreat, and two or three weeks for summer vacation.

A laywoman who was not married explained how she was able to supplement her salary in order to meet expenses.

> I found it necessary to supplement the salary they could offer me here because of the fact of having left religious life at the age of thirty-nine, and not having any income accrued for retirement. So to do that, it was part of the agreement that I established with the parish from the outset and also with the bishop, that that would be the only way I could consider doing this, if I could supplement my income by doing additional ministry. Originally I wanted to put in the equivalent of about ten hours a week [in additional ministry], but I found that was impossible, so I cut back to approximately six hours a week.

Only ten percent (2) of the parishes I visited were situated in urban areas; the rest were located in small parishes in rural towns or villages. Thirty-five percent (7) of the parishes were in towns with populations of 1,000 to 9,999; and the largest percentage, fifty-five percent (11) were in towns or villages with populations under one thousand.

One of the priest interviewees was critical of the policy of placing women to head small parishes in small rural areas. He said,

> I was a little disappointed in the sense that if the diocese is going to make a commitment about women in ministry, I felt it was wrong that they started here [in a small parish]. Now they talked about it in two veins. One was the role of women. They wanted to encourage women in ministry. And then a second area was the shortage of priests. Well, if they're going to deal with the shortage of priest problem, they should have put (the woman pastor), or any other sister, at the Cathedral parish, a big parish. I mean, that would make a statement. This was not a statement parish, so I felt it was kind of a weak statement on their part that we're really concerned about putting women in the roles of ministry. If they really wanted to, they would have picked a larger parish, I think, with more visibility.

Table 2 summarizes the characteristics of the parishes. The average amount of experience as a pastoral administrator is four years, and the range is from one year to eight. Eighteen of the women are pastoring for the first time; two of them had served at another parish prior to this, their second appointment.

Table 2
Characteristics of Parishes

	*Census Region**	*Population***	*Parish Size****	*Race/Ethnicity*
1.	West	Small Urban	Small	White
2.	West	Medium Rural	Medium	Mexican-Amer.
3.	South	Small Rural	Medium	White
4.	South	Medium Rural	Large	Black
5.	South	Large Urban	Large	White/Black
6.	Midwest	Small Rural	Medium	White
7.	Midwest	Small Rural	Medium	White
8.	Midwest	Small Rural	Medium	White
9.	Midwest	Small Rural	Small	White
10.	Midwest	Small Rural	Medium	White
11.	Midwest	Small Rural	Medium	White
12.	Midwest	Small Rural	Small	White
13.	Northeast	Small Rural	Medium	White
14.	Northeast	Medium Rural	Large	White
15.	West	Medium Rural	Small	White
16.	South	Medium Rural	Large	Mexican-Amer.
17.	South	Small Rural	Medium	White
18.	South	Small Rural	Small	White
19.	West	Medium Rural	Medium	White
10.	West	Medium Rural	Large	White/Mex.-Amer.

* Northeast (Middle Atlantic and New England); Midwest (East and West North Central); South (East and West South Central and South Atlantic); West (Mountain and Pacific).
**Large Urban (over 250,000); Small Urban (10,000 to 49,999); Medium Rural (1,000–9,999); Small Rural (Under 1,000).
***Large (200+ families); Medium (100–199 families); Small (Under 100 families).

Thus far we have explored some of the background characteristics of the women pastors, their recruitment processes, and the general context of the parishes they are heading. Now I want to complete the portrait of these women by looking at their personal characteristics as seen by them, by their parishioners, and by their sacramental ministers.

PERSONAL CHARACTERISTICS

One of the descriptive words used often by parishioners when they are referring to their woman pastor is "approachable." A female parishioner who had four years of experience with her pastor said,

> She is just so easy to work with and approach when you have something you don't like or want to talk to her about. She is so receptive and much easier to talk to.... I had never done that before with a priest. That's my point of view and I am sure that is shared by others.

A male parishioner in the same parish said,

> She is available every day and we can always call her. She is so close. The priest, either he was gone on business, or [at] a meeting.

The previous resident priests, in many cases, had been ill and therefore less approachable. As one of the women pastors explained,

> The last two [resident priests] were very old and very ill, and they were really not pastors. In fact, the last one was so ill that when he said Mass the last three years he was here, two men had to support him at the altar, stand on either side of him and hold him up. And he never gave a homily.

A female parishioner said she felt that her pastor's administrative skills and knowledge were less important in the adjustment to her new role than the fact that she was compassionate and patient when she interacted with parishioners. She argued that these personal qualities made the woman pastor more approachable, and thus more effective.

One of the sacramental ministers used the term "click" when he described the approachability of a woman pastor who had previously served in the parish as a pastoral associate.

They knew her before; that helped. But the key has been her personality. I believe that just as individuals click or don't click that the same thing happens for parishes and priests or administrators. Either they click or they don't, and I think with [the woman pastor] it clicked. She was secure enough as an individual not to take the nonacceptance as personal. She was secure enough; she was patient enough. She fits with the community because the community is very, very down-to-earth and she is down-to-earth. So it has worked for a whole bunch of reasons.

The woman parishioners were especially effusive about the approachability of their women pastors. Having a pastor who could understand from experience what it meant to be a mother, daughter, or sister was a new experience for them. One woman stopped me after Mass on Sunday, and with tears in her eyes told me that her pastor had helped her through some very difficult times, and had been like a sister to her. I observed the approachability of the woman pastor "in action" on several occasions during my parish visits when I saw the parishioners enthusiastically approach her before and after Mass at the entrance of the church, at wedding receptions, at local community gatherings, at restaurants while we were eating dinner, and on the streets of her town or village as she gave me a guided tour. On the other hand, one or two of the women pastors were not as approachable as the others, and parishioners were not afraid to voice their concern about it. One of the female parishioners said, "I would like to see (her pastor) handle people a little smoother. I feel bad for her because she does make enemies because of her abruptness."

In another parish one of the male parishioners said he felt that his woman pastor could still learn to be "a little more tactful in getting people to do what they ought to do." He said that when she first took over she had to go through the process of learning that "you don't treat volunteers the same way you do military people." He said she had to learn that these people "were willing to give their time, but they weren't willing to be pushed around." He quoted another male parishioner's reaction to her tactics who said, "The next time that bossy bitch tells me I have to do something, I am going to tell her to take a flying leap and take my kids to another church."

Learning to combine approachability with a measure of toughness did not come easy for some of these women. One of them described her confrontation with a male parishioner at a parish council meeting during her first year on the job.

> I said, "Let's stop right here. First of all, you do not speak to me in this tone of voice. I will not take that ever again." Well, he got up and said, "I'm going to get out of here and I'm leaving this parish, and I'm taking a whole bunch of families with me." And he stormed out. And I said, "God knows what I've done now."

Even though his family may have stayed away for a short time, they soon returned to the parish and became active again. The fact that she took a stand with him went down well with the parishioners, as a male parishioner attested:

> She handled it very well. I can remember times at a council meeting when she had to be very tactful in dealing with some of the people who had been on the council for years. In my opinion, she handled it very well. She was really patient. She was firm, and can be very firm, but I think just being intelligent and patient and understanding of what the situation was.

One of the women pastors reflected on the need to deemphasize the virtue of humility, especially in the beginning:

> If I could do it over I would exude more self-confidence, take a stronger role in the beginning, not be afraid of being called pastor. I think I had a hang-up about that, that that was prestigious, and I shouldn't be going around making myself important or something.

Another personality dimension often mentioned was introvert and extrovert. Because the "good pastor" is depicted as one who is outgoing, the introverts tend to have a more difficult time adjusting to the role. One of the sacramental ministers explained why the woman pastor was reluctant to visit the homes of parishioners.

> We've had a number of conversations about Myers-Briggs.[7] We've talked about that, and on the Myers-Briggs she certainly is an introvert. She shared with me that she's not overly comfortable in that kind of setting, going into the home and sitting

down and having a cup of coffee, and some people are. But she finds that very difficult. So I'm not sure if it's exactly because she's an introvert. It may be more her formal style, too, that you don't go to someone's house unless you're invited, and then it's okay to stop by.

One of the women who was having trouble adjusting to her role as pastor said,

Myers-Briggs checks me out as an introvert. I don't like talking in front of people. I'm not comfortable with it. If you are not comfortable, you don't do a good job. I am getting better. Obviously I can't get any worse, but it isn't my thing.

One of the women pastors described herself as an introvert with "a tendency to internalize a lot of the feelings that come from negative presence and vibrations." As I watched her preside at a word and communion service one Sunday, and observed how well she communicated with the congregation, it was difficult to view her as an introvert.

Another woman pastor who had been an aspiring actress earlier in her life, told me that she still teams up with a friend to put on a comedy routine for parties and special occasions that "has people falling over with laughter." Although I was unable to observe her in action, I was told that she often receives applause from the parishioners after she preaches.

Another example comes from an extroverted woman pastor:

I feel that through these other experiences I got to know how to approach people, how to be available to people, how to be more aware of needs. And especially I think this is very much a part of my temperament, but I like working with all this. I hate doing things by myself. In my religious life, it was kind of a difficult situation, because in the old times you were supposed to fulfill everything [yourself], and I always like to do things with other people, teamwork.

This view of some of the personal characteristics of the women pastors completes the portrait of the women and their parishes. We turn in the next chapter to a discussion of a quality unique to these women, the "pastoral heart."

·3·

The Pastoral Heart

The word "pastoral" comes from the Latin *pastoralis,* meaning "of or relating to herdsman or shepherd," and in a religious context the word "pastor" has come to mean a "spiritual overseer; especially a clergyman serving a local church or parish."[1] In the Christian tradition the gospel account of the good shepherd portrays the ideal characteristics for a pastor, whose "flock" consists of his parishioners. The pertinent scriptural passages from the Gospel of John (10:2–3, 14) are the following:

> The one who enters through the gate is the shepherd of the flock; the gatekeeper lets him in, the sheep hear his voice, one by one he calls his own sheep and leads them out.... I am the good shepherd; I know my own and my own know me...[2]

One of the key ingredients for a good shepherd is his intimate knowledge of his flock which enables him to call each of his sheep by name. As a result of this familiarity, the sheep recognize his voice and follow him. In this scriptural passage we are not told how the shepherd becomes familiar with his flock, but we can imagine that he had to spend a considerable amount of time and effort in distinguishing one from another.

Note how the masculine gender predominates in this English translation of the scriptural passage. Just as the word "shepherd" calls forth the image of a man with his sheep, so does the term "pastor" conjure up the image of a man with his parishioners. Interestingly enough, there is a feminine term, "shepherdess," that is well known, but the word "pastoress" is not commonly used. No wonder, then, that people have difficulty picturing a woman in charge of a parish!

The title for this chapter came from an incident in one of the parishes I visited, that captured a quality of these women pastors. This characteristic was something that the parishioners mentioned again and again. When they described how she interacted with them, parishioners usually began by stating that first of all, she knew their names, and they deeply appreciated her calling them by name.

Secondly, the parishioners mentioned the fact that she went out of her way to visit them in their homes and to spend time in their family settings. Thirdly, they treasured her visits to sick and dying parishioners both at home and in the hospital. Finally, the parishioners cherished their warm relationships with her.

All of the information from these parishioners' testimonies could be embodied in the term "pastoral heart," a term that I first heard in an interview with a woman pastor who was quoting a bishop when he was presiding at a meeting with the pastors of his diocese. The bishop had just returned from a confirmation ceremony held the previous day in her parish where he had accompanied her on a visit to a little girl who was dying of cancer. He had been deeply touched by this experience, and it was evident in his talk to the pastors. The following is the woman pastor's account of the meeting.

> The next day we were at a deanery[3] meeting and he started making his remarks and [said], "Yesterday I had the opportunity to visit a family and a little girl," and he described what the disease was doing to them. And he said, "But I could tell, as I was there, the interaction between Sister and the family, how much love and care there is between them and how much a support they are to each other. And that's what I mean when I talk about having a pastoral heart."

She continued,

> He used that as an example. I wasn't expecting him to say it. I didn't even know he was observing me. That kind of thing I don't think he sees that much among his priests. So I think it's a different dimension that women, in general, bring to it.

The "different dimension" was also attested to by one of her parishioners, who said,

> Any family you talk to, in their bad moments you can feel the good that they feel when she walks in. We just had a little girl who died a month or so ago and she did everything she possibly could with that family. She even stayed with the children. She really went out of her way.

Seldom did any of the women pastors discuss their strategies for living out the ideals of the pastoral heart. But this dimension was a constant in every parish I visited. I saw it lived out as I followed them around during the weekend. I read about it in some of the parish evaluation sheets I perused. It fairly shouted at me when I read the weekly church bulletins composed by them, and I heard parishioners and priests alike attest to it. There was one woman who spoke of it as a strategy for women newly appointed as pastoral administrators. The following is her advice to women who are considering an acceptance of an appointment to a priestless parish:

> Talk to people in the beginning. Live with them for a weekend. Just move around with them for awhile. And when you get to the place, the first thing is to be friendly with the people. Do that before you make any other moves. That's so important because you have to gain their trust. If you don't have their trust, you can turn the world upside down and they aren't going to like you. You have to win their hearts.

Why the need for such strategy? It could be their gender and/or their lay status that causes women pastors to look for ways to win the parishioners' hearts. It could also be that any new pastor would be inclined to utilize this strategy. Both are partial answers.

As we saw in the last chapter, most of the women pastors had previously performed the nurturant role of teacher. However, even the laywomen who had functioned in and competed successfully in a "man's world"—the military, business, etc.—and of necessity had taken on more "male" characteristics *also* perceived the need for the "pastoral heart," and strove to realize it.

Perhaps the newcomer status of these women combined with their position as laity and as women prompted them to develop the characteristics of the pastoral heart. What must be kept in mind is that all of the previous pastors in their parishes were clergy, so these women were not the kind of replacement that Catholic parishioners would expect or, indeed, want. Time and again I heard references to a "grieving process" that many parishioners experienced, and I saw references to it in articles on pastoral ministry. Evidently, losing the parish priest is like a death in the family for some parishioners, so the newly arrived woman pastor finds that she must work harder than any previous pastor to win the hearts of her parishioners.

These women initially had two strikes against them: their gender and the fact that they were replacing a priest in a nontraditional context. But the reason so many of them scored instead of striking out was that they went out of their way to learn the names of their parishioners and called them by name, they visited their homes and got to know the family situation, and they did all of this in a warm and caring way. In short, their words and actions embodied the pastoral heart. In the remainder of this chapter I will elaborate on these three characteristics of the pastoral heart: naming, visiting, and personal warmth.

NAMING PEOPLE

The ability to call people by name is an important one. Naming confers or at least implies validation of the person. To name someone suggests familiarity, but it also underlines the worth of the individual. In the context of this study, when the pastor calls her parishioners by name, it means not only that she is including them as esteemed members of the parish, but she is also acknowledging their gifts to the community.

When I visited these parishes, I made it a point to arrive early for the Sunday Masses, and to stand outside the church afterwards to observe the interaction between the woman pastor and her parishioners. Typically she would be standing outside both before and after the service, greeting each parishioner by name, and asking about other members of the family. Later on during Mass, when she helped to distribute communion, she also called each communicant by name.

In some parishes she would announce the names of those

with birthdays or anniversaries during the coming week, and the parishioners would sing to them. In one instance, each child was invited to come forward to receive a small birthday gift. One young teenager beamed when he was congratulated by the pastor during her announcements at the end of Sunday Mass for having been elected the president of his class.

One of the female parishioners described how her pastor made a public announcement every Sunday of the names of parish helpers:

> One of the things that [she] does is announce right before the Mass begins who they (the congregation) are going to be seeing visually—the eucharistic ministers, the altar boys, the choir, the celebrant, the lectors, the people bringing up the gifts—by name. It is important that everybody knows everybody in our parish, maybe not by name, but as a member of (our parish), and a conversation starts. And they realize how much they have in common once they start talking.

One could argue that the parish bulletin typically includes the names of the persons who are performing these tasks, so this oral announcement really is not necessary. And that is indeed true—for those few parishioners who already know everyone in the parish. But for the majority who do not, the added effort to point the person out by name can serve as a weekly "getting to know you" exercise.

Even more important, the oral announcement can also function as as an occasion when family members can point with pride to their relatives who are serving on the altar on that particular Sunday. I observed some of this family reaction when I saw parishioners smile and nudge one another at the announcement of a family member's name. They not only appreciated the public recognition, but it was a confirmation that they, the parishioners, were important to the working of the parish.

The oral announcement is also consistent with the conviction voiced again and again by the women pastors—that each person's gift should be acknowledged. One of them described a strategy she used to accomplish this:

> We are having an Appreciation Day, and I want to name every single person. So there would be parish council, all of the

commissions, the administration committee, the cemetery committee, the people that clean the church, the person that sends the bulletin to the shut-ins, the person who calls the family mid-week to remind them that they are bringing up the Offertory gifts. There are the eucharistic ministers, the lectors, the youth ministers, the religious education teachers. It goes on and on.

How does she learn all of their names? In one parish of five hundred the pastor showed me the calendar hanging in her kitchen where she had inserted the names of each parishioner's birthday, and said she tries to remember to wish them a happy birthday. Another had a picture of each parishioner with their names inserted on their birthdays on a large calendar on her desk.

The parishioners responded with gratitude to these efforts. A male parishioner said,

> I think she knows just about everybody and their kids on a first-name basis. She is always going out of her way to meet you. She worked hard to get to know everybody. Every Mass she stood outside, no matter how cold or hot it was, trying to get to know everybody on a first-name basis, so her efforts were apparent.

Another male parishioner described his pastor this way:

> She gets involved with everybody. She knows everybody's name. She knows who you are, where you live, what you do for a living, what your needs are, and so on. She is very, very much a part of the community.

Another parishioner said that he thought the people in his parish gave her more support than the previous pastor "because I think Father _____ had a tendency to forget names. He kind of drove some people away because he didn't remember names."

One of the women pastors said it took her awhile to figure out why it was that everybody was zipping in the back door each weekend, without even looking at her. She explained,

> I think I figured out Father _____ did not take time to learn people's names. He didn't know their names. I think people don't feel important enough to be spoken to. You know how when you don't know somebody's name, and you are too embarrassed to ask. So they zipped past.

Not all priest-pastors have a tendency to forget names, of course, but it is impossible for most priests who are serving as many as three parishes to learn the names of all the parishioners. In several of the parishes I visited the priests had to leave immediately after Mass in order to reach the next parish in time. One priest, in fact, went right into the sacristy after Mass, took off his vestments, and jumped into his car without a word. So they tend to adopt an attitude like the sacramental minister who gave me the following rationale for avoiding a "divided heart" situation:

> I don't know these people's names. I know their faces and something about them, and there are a few over four years I've begun to recognize. But I have never given my heart to this community, on purpose. My heart belongs over there [in his parish]. I worked that out. I have gotten criticized by parishioners here because I end every Mass in [my parish] by saying, "I love you, have a good day." And I do that on purpose. I don't say that here. That's not my role here. That is Sister's position—to be the heart of the community.

To this priest, knowing the names of the people, calling them by name, and showing affection for them were necessary actions if the pastor was to take his or her position as the heart of the community. One of the priests I interviewed testified to the success of a woman pastor in this regard, and described a recent reaction of the local bishop to a woman pastor's winning way in the community.

> I think [she] has won over the hearts of the people up there [at her parish]. I think they have a genuine affection for her. She has many important gifts. She can call almost everyone by their first name. At confirmation last Saturday she had thirty kids and she just called them all by name, one by one, and asked them to stand as she called their names to introduce them to the bishop. That's very impressive. The bishop was impressed. He leaned over to me and said, "She's not using a list." And I said, "She isn't, Bishop." And he said, "Not very often can the pastor do that."

Not every woman pastor was as effective with regard to naming, however. One parishioner whom I interviewed expressed her concern about this. She wanted her pastor to be more outgoing and caring, and to call the parishioners by name more often. In fact, she pinpointed the pastor's failure to be able to name her parishioners as a key problem in the parish at the present time.

Naming their parishioners will undoubtedly become more and more difficult for priest-pastors who, because of the clergy shortage, are increasingly being assigned to serve more than one parish. It is not only sheer numbers that stand in their way, but also the hours spent in travel leave less time for parishioners on a day-to-day basis. Eighteen of the twenty parishes had sacramental ministers (priests) who traveled to one, two, or even three other parishes to celebrate Mass on a weekend. In the remaining two cases, the sacramental ministers were elderly priests who had come out of retirement to help the woman pastor. They were physically unable to serve more than one parish.

By contrast, only five of the women pastors were administering more than one parish or mission, and three more were helping out part-time in another parish in only one program, for example in the liturgy or religious education programs. Like the circuit-riding priests, these women found that they had less time to learn names, and fewer opportunities to address parishioners by name. The divided commitment also cut into the time they would have preferred to spend in visiting parishioners' homes.

VISITING PARISHIONERS

In a certain sense, visiting parishioners at home or in the hospital can be seen as a way to achieve a deeper understanding of them, beyond the naming stage. These visits might also function as a way to write the names of the parishioners indelibly on one's memory. The sharing of parishioners' experiences in their own living environments could also serve to bring the parishioners' joys and sorrows into the weekly sermons. As one woman pastor said, in explaining why she spent time with parish teenagers, "I need to be in touch with what's going on and I need to hear their stories."

Other than pastors, what other professionals are expected to make home visits in today's society? For many Americans a home visit by the family doctor is a thing of the past. Even patients being treated in hospitals complain about not seeing their own doctors very often. Welfare workers could be listed, but their visits are limited to only one segment of society. In addition, the brief, formally bureaucratic, and therefore alienating visits of the welfare worker are a far cry from the visits expected of pastors.

Women pastors interviewed cited the visiting of parishioners as a top priority, and parishioner appreciation of this effort was a recurring theme. The following statements illustrate this:

> From talking to her and observing, I think she spends quite a bit of time one-on-one with people, visiting. She likes to do that, plus from what I have heard, people that are in need and need someone to talk to or need counseling like to talk to [her].

Many of the pastors visited every single home in the parish during the first year of their appointment. In one such parish a parishioner said,

> When they see her come up to their house, they enjoy seeing her coming, especially the older people. And the young kids— my daughter really likes to see her come to the house. We always invite her when we celebrate birthdays or anniversaries. And then the whole family gets to meet her.
>
> She works with the poor people and the sick people of the parish. She is always there. Anytime of the day you call her, if somebody is sick in the parish, like [when] I had surgery, she came to stay with the family. She does things that people don't expect, but she does them out of the goodness of her heart.
>
> Just to give you an example, my mother was in ICU just before she died. She thought the world of [the woman pastor]. [She] was just going through [town] during the week and decided to stop, and when Mama opened her eyes and recognized her, Mama said, "I hadn't realized it was Sunday." She would associate [the woman pastor] with communion. Mama was almost out of it but she still recognized her.

Many parishioners compared her visits with that of former pastors, as in the following:

> I think [she] is more available to the people. The priests we have had, they were there, but the attitude was the people come to them. They had office hours and would schedule them.

In the beginning she had big shoes to fill. We had had a parish priest who was here four or five years and he was like a member of all of our families, and when he left it was hard. She has become that same type of person who is irreplaceable in our hearts.

Priests likewise attested to the priority placed by these women on visiting parishioners. One of the priests described a woman pastor's reaction when she received the news that a twenty-year-old parishioner, working in another part of the country, had committed suicide.

As soon as she found out she called me and said, "I think they need a priest out there. Would you like to go along?" I said, "Pick me up and I'll be ready." We went out there and we didn't really do much except sit there and be with the people. They were just in shock. So we sat there for about an hour and a half and [the woman pastor] made coffee and we hugged and kissed everybody and sat around. Afterwards I found out that [she] had gone out there every day after that to be with the family. It was a whole week before they got the body here. We got the news on a Thursday night and the wake was the next Thursday. So she was very supportive. And they know that.

In a similar vein, another priest said,

She visits the sick very well. I am amazed of her knowledge of everybody, all the families, who is sick. She is just wonderful with being on top of what is going on in the people's lives here, and she seems to visit a whole lot.

Another priest, by contrast, was concerned that the woman pastor, who was experiencing a number of stresses in her life, was finding it difficult to make home visits. He said,

But pastorally, probably [she] struggles with being comfortable in the home situation. Now this could be a cultural thing with coming from [the city] or it could just be a personality thing. Some people are very comfortable walking into somebody's kitchen and sitting down and having a cup of coffee. And a lot of church happens in that context. There aren't many farmers left in the parish who are running active farms, but the farm mentality and rural mentality is here. People choose to live isolated, and I think their world is their home, more than people who live in a city where the neighborhood might be more significant and people may be more outgoing in city living. So a lot of church, I believe, happens here over a cup of coffee. So that aspect is lacking a bit.

One of the circuit-riding sacramental ministers expressed his own frustrations about "skimming through" people's lives.

As far as my own feelings about that go, I think it is more [a matter of] dealing with my own frustration at not being able to do some of the things that I really enjoy about the priesthood. The biggest problem that we face that colors everything we do is the amount of driving. It's an hour and forty-five minutes from one end of the parish to another. Yesterday and today I was out visiting people and did sixty miles round-trip. So I figure we spend an average [of] seven to ten forty-hour work-weeks just driving. So that limits what you do. And when I do have free time I am so glad to have a night off I don't want to see anybody. So what I end up doing is skim through people's lives. It takes three times as long to get to know your parishioners when you have them in two or three communities.

Another priest who was, in general, very impressed and highly supportive of the woman pastor, felt that the parish was, in a certain sense, being shortchanged because, although she was living in the parish just a few blocks from the church, she chose not to live in the rectory. He stressed the importance of availability as well as visiting, and he described her predecessor this way:

He was quite popular, had been there [in the parish] for a long time, lived there, interacted with the people…was involved with families in a hundred different kinds of ways. Really involved in people's lives. He lived alone, had no community life to sustain him, and [was] available twenty-four hours.

The description above would fit only two of the immediate predecessors of the women interviewed. As one of the women pastors put it, "Most priests want the people to come to them. We go out to the people." This same woman described an exchange with her predecessor—a retired priest from another diocese—that occurred while she was serving in her present parish as a parish associate in charge of religious education.

I think it was a little too much for him to be here. He was very
lonely, he didn't want to go around and visit families. I would
tell him, "Father, go and visit people." And he would say, "No,
because they don't invite me." I told him, "Father, people don't
work this way. You go out to them and then they will start
inviting you." But it didn't work out. He started getting very
defensive because I was many times telling him, "Father, I
don't think this is the right way to do it."

To understand these older priests, their seminary experiences
before Vatican II must be appreciated. The other-worldly spiritu-
ality that prevailed in that era dictated a cautious attitude regarding the visiting of parishioners. They were warned about "playing favorites," and about adopting surrogate families, thus
causing divisiveness in the parish. In particular they were
warned not to visit only those parishioners who invited them to
come for a meal, for that would exclude those who couldn't
afford a meal that would be "fitting" for a priest.

One of the women who had been pastoring for four years
was commenting on an article analyzing the impact of Vatican II
on priests, where the author stressed the idea of a priest visiting
every home in the parish at least once a year. She said,

In the hearts of the people, that's what they really want. My
hunch is that most people don't care about what goes on at
parish council, don't care about what goes on in finance council, but their stories are, "I remember when Father So-and-So
came over and did such and such," or "He was at the hospital," or "He came to our reception."

Many of the women pastors began the home visits almost
immediately upon their arrival at the parish, because it helped
them to learn the parishioners' names. One of them who also
used her camera as a strategy described her visits thus:

The thing that helped was that I went around and visited every
household. I also took pictures when I went. I had a little routine when I went to the house. I said, "I brought my camera. I
want to take your picture because on my desk I have a little
flip photograph album, and every day I turn the page and
that's the household, and those are the people I remember at
Mass." So those kinds of little things were impressive to the
people. I always gave them a copy of the photograph.

Several of them described incidents when parishioners called on them, rather than the priest [sacramental minister], in time of need:

> About three months ago, it was late, about 10:30, and I was on the phone. The operator interrupted the call and asked if I could please hang up, that there was an emergency. So I did, and immediately one of our parishioners called and said, "Could you come out right away? Grandma is very, very sick. We don't know what is going to happen." And I said, "Yes, I'll be glad to. Do you want me to call Father?" "Oh yeah, maybe you could." They called me first. It wasn't even on their mind to call Father.

Another woman pastor also attested to being called instead of the priest:

> As far as death, there is so much to being with a person or with the family when someone dies that the priest is not there for anyway. I am there at that time. Father comes in and puts a little oil on them, but he usually does that six months or more before they die. I am the one who brings them eucharist every week. I am the one who is with them or helps the family. I was the one that when [a young parishioner] died, they called me. She died real early in the morning. She was getting worse and had a little coughing spell. They had nurses around the clock in the home because they wanted to keep her in the home to make her as comfortable as they could. She was unconscious most of those last few days. I would stop in and I would talk to her when I would be there because I still felt like she could hear. They didn't call the priest to tell him. They called me.

This same woman explained why she felt that women pastors' attitudes about visiting parishioners were different from those of their predecessors when she said, "I think there is more of a going out to people, a caring for people."

Not everyone finds it easy to visit people in the hospital, especially when they are at the point of death.[4] During one parish visit, shortly after Sunday Mass, the woman pastor received a call from the daughter of a parishioner who was in the hospital with cancer. The family thought the ninety-four-year-old woman was near death, so the pastor decided to go. I accompanied her and the priest to the hospital. The priest recited the opening prayers, and then the woman pastor spoke to and blessed the dying woman, who showed signs of recognizing her. About halfway through the administration of the sacrament, the woman pastor left the room because, as she explained afterward, she was feeling ill. Nonetheless, she returned shortly thereafter. In the car on the way home, she told me that she finds it very difficult to be present at a death, and this is not one of her favorite duties. Who, after all, looks forward to such an occasion?

The final example regarding the practice of reaching out to parishioners comes from a woman pastor's reaction when she heard that some of the parishioners were disturbed because they heard that the parish council was considering a replacement for the old altar in the church. Although this was a seemingly insignificant issue, she went to the home of an elderly parishioner to speak to her personally because she sensed that the woman needed reassurance. In her words,

> When I heard that there was this one lady who was really kind of upset about it, I went to her house and I said I heard she was upset. And she said she was wondering why, so I told her why. I said, "Well, first of all, the other one is cracked and in need of repair. And, secondly, the tabernacle should not be on the altar; it should be separate." She said, "Well, that's good then. If that's the way it's supposed to be, I guess that's the way we ought to do it." It was kind of the sentimental value of the old one, but once you gave her a reasonable explanation, it was fine.

Although the reason for this visit was not the physical suffering of a parishioner, and thus could perhaps have been dismissed as not critical, nonetheless the woman pastor responded, and the visit had a healing effect. The visit itself was not sufficient for the healing; it was the way the pastor interacted with her once she arrived. In addition to naming people and visiting parishioners, the pastoral heart requires a third ingredient—personal warmth.

PERSONAL WARMTH

When parishioners described their pastors, invariably the word "warm" emerged in the conversation. I observed many examples of their personal warmth in the pastors' responses to parishioners in a variety of settings. On the two occasions when I accompanied them to visit dying parishioners, I was struck by the pastor's sensitivity to pain, and the loving way she conducted the ritual. The way they greeted people who rang the doorbell at the parish house, their readiness to embrace parishioners at social gatherings, and sometimes just the eagerness with which parishioners approached them—all were outward signs of the personal warmth of these women. Even inside the church itself they would often give members of the congregation warm hugs as they extended the kiss of peace prior to the distribution of Communion during a service. Their caring is evidenced in some of the following statements by parishioners:

> When [she] came, she actually knit the parish closer together. It did happen. People got to know her, respect her and love her. Now, if she leaves, I don't know what's going to happen. The older people got to love her so much. When she is not down there Saturday night at Mass, there is something missing.
>
> [She] is there for every Mass. She is the first one there and is always at the door saying, "Hi," hugging, greeting people.

In eighteen of the twenty parishes parishioners expressed their appreciation for the warm and outgoing manner of their pastors. They feel "very close" to her. Many said, "She's one of us."

Priests also testified to the personal warmth of these women. One of them said, "She is hugged and kissed before and after Mass by everybody every week." Another priest, reflecting on this aspect of her ministry, said,

> I think people are touched by her. And, in a way, I would guess, too, they would not be and probably could not be by a man, by a priest. What I sense is that she is able to plug in, to express or open up or invite a different part of people than what probably most priests would touch. I don't know if this will sound contrived, but to me it is the feminine level of life. She even talks different. The words she uses are different than the words I use. She is able to feel more what especially the women of the parish—what's happening to them and within them and their life, and the experiences they are having. I think she is able to identify better with that. And also with men, in some ways.

Another priest who was comparing the woman pastor with her immediate predecessor said that she had "much more warmth in her dealings with people. And I just think she has a better concept of being a pastor."

One evening at a parish "ice cream social" held in the church basement immediately after the Saturday evening Mass, there was a good example of the different stances of priest and woman pastor. The woman pastor joined right in with the parishioners, kidding them, and accepting their joking in a very friendly way. In contrast, the priest kept himself aloof. His clothing and bearing did not invite informal interaction from the parishioners. In fact, his behavior on that occasion contradicted what he had told me earlier regarding his eagerness to be with the parishioners, and how much he enjoyed the interaction with them. He was not very outgoing in this instance, and had he chosen to wear a sportshirt rather than a Roman collar, he might have mingled more easily. In contrast, the woman pastor's clothing, a summery dress with a white jacket, blended with the parishioners' dress.

During Mass on weekends when the sacramental minister was presiding and the woman pastor was present, I often wrote in my field notes how much warmer and more outgoing was she than he. Parishioners, too, made those comparisons. A male parishioner said,

> I think, rightly or wrongly, that [she] should be our priest. That's how I feel about it. I have no other feeling. My mother died last January, and [she] was a great comfort to us. I love Father _____; don't misunderstand me. But we are here, this is our locale, she is the person here; she should be taking care of us.

A female parishioner put it this way,

> I feel very comfortable with [her] as a woman being administrator and counselor and everything else, the whole ball of wax that she is. I feel a woman has more empathy and understanding of a lot of things that are happening in home life and parish life that a man can't understand and be sympathetic to. I think it's made a difference and would make a big difference in the whole country.

In fairness to the priests who are serving as sacramental ministers, it is important to remember that they are not the resident priest in the parishes I visited. Instead they are "visitors" in these situations, and resident pastors only in their own parishes, so their own parishioners are their first priority. Thus part of the explanation for the failure of some of the priests to be as outgoing as the women I visited was due to their extensive travel schedules. The role of circuit riding sacramental minister depleted the energy needed by these priests to extend themselves to parishioners.

Because parishioners value personal warmth in their woman pastor, they tend to be disappointed when they fail to see it displayed by them. One parishioner complained about the lack of warmth in her pastor. She was especially disappointed because her pastor did not make it a point to greet people individually before Mass.

> She greets them as a whole [in the church], like "Good evening." But she will be running back and forth to and from the sacristy, and passes people and doesn't acknowledge their presence. Again, I don't think it's deliberate. Maybe she thinks they won't respond back, I don't know. But that means a lot to those people.

On the other hand, women pastors were concerned about the response of the parishioners to their displays of warmth, especially during the first year of their appointment, when their acceptance is in question. One woman, who was appointed head of an Hispanic parish explained,

> In the Spanish tradition, especially with the male, you would know if you were accepted if you received the *abrazo,* which was a chestlike hug. I guess in American slang we call it a big bear hug. And you were pummeled on your back. When you got that, you knew you were in, because there was an intimacy to that. It was an acceptance. It was very public so it was sending a message to the community. I waited about eight months until I got that from the head usher. When I got that I floated on air. I knew I had arrived.

One of the pastors I visited was especially good at combining a personal warmth with a strong sense of justice. She had a wonderful open and loving way with her parishioners. For instance, she was a great "hugger," and also loved to tease and joke with her parishioners. But she was also a realistic and confronting pastor. For instance, she continued to counsel the young people in her parish who dropped out of school, repeating over and over again, "You can *do* it." She expressed the deep sadness she felt when "her kids" got pregnant or took drugs because she is so convinced that they can and must break out of the cycle of poverty. She took every opportunity to affirm the individual personhood of her parishioners.

Up to this point we have examined the characteristics of the pastoral heart from the vantage points of parishioner, priest, and woman pastor. In the final section of this chapter we look at some of the effects of this phenomenon for parishes.

CONSEQUENCES FOR THE PARISH

During the Mass or communion service, there is one moment called the "kiss of peace," when the consequence of the pastor's naming, visiting, and personal warmth was acted out in the ritual. At this point in the service, after the "Our Father" is recited, and just before the distribution of Communion, the person who presides says, "Let us offer each other the sign of peace." Parishioners then usually shake hands with those on either side of them, and the priest may come down from the altar and shake hands with a few parishioners. This whole "event" usually takes just a few minutes in most parishes.

In parishes with women pastors, however, this "moment" stretches out in many directions. First, there was hugging and kissing as well as shaking hands by both parishioners and presiders. Secondly, the woman invariably came down from the sanctuary and literally made the rounds of the entire congregation. If the sacramental minister was presiding, both he and the pastor might come down from the altar, and each would cover half the congregation, shaking hands or hugging each person on his or her side of the church. Thirdly, parishioners did not limit their greetings to those people standing on either side of them. Often, everyone around them, and even those located in other parts of the church, would receive their handshake, hug, and/or kiss.

Several of the women pastors would ask visitors from outside the parish to identify themselves before Mass began, or just before they announced the kiss of peace, so that parishioners could greet the visitors by name. Needless to say, the enactment of this joyous moment often took a good deal of time.

In one parish, for example, the choir and the congregation repeated many verses of the song "Reach Out and Touch Somebody's Hand," during the kiss of peace, because most of the parishioners moved out of their pews to greet people in other parts of the church, and the priest and pastor each greeted every single person, about eighty in all. At the very end of Mass the woman pastor thanked me publicly for visiting the parish, and invited me to come to the center of the church so that the members of the congregation could give me their blessing. All joined in singing their version of "Aaron's Blessing," with their right hands extended toward me. They were allowing me to share their spirit of community for a short time.[5]

One priest testified to the "great spirit of family" that had been built up in the parish in the two years since the arrival of the lay pastor:

> There are certain things that...you notice is giving you clues as to the spirit of the parish. One is how long and how many people hang around after Mass on Sunday at the door. If they all disappear right away, there is not much of a sense of community in the parish. Here I have noticed more and more people who are standing outside and talking.

How is the parish affected by a parish leader who lives out the characteristics of a pastoral heart? Probably the most important consequence of the willingness of the pastor to name people, to visit parishioners, and to interact in a warm personal manner is a growing sense of community throughout the parish. It is exemplified in moments like the extended sign of peace ritual, in the smiles of parishioners as they greet each other outside the church, the hours of voluntary service they contribute to the parish, and in the sacrifices they make in another parishioner's hour of need.

•4•

Collaborative Leadership

One of the striking differences between the women pastors and their predecessors is their collaborative leadership style. A collaborative relationship, where all of the persons in the group or organization work together jointly to achieve a common end, is based on equality rather than hierarchy. In a collaborative relationship, one individual works *with,* not *for* another.

Is the label "collaborative leadership," then, a contradiction in terms? It may be a contradiction if leadership means a relationship in which one person has the commanding authority or influence, and others are expected to obey her or his commands. In a parish situation this would mean that parishioners are basically passive rather than active participants, and the principal actor, or "leader," is the pastor.

On the other hand, if leadership means a relationship where the leader guides rather than commands, and in so doing, draws on the talents of others, then collaborative leadership is possible. This means that parishioners take part in activities that have an impact on the parish and are not confined merely to sitting in the pews on Sunday.[1] This is basically how women pastors define their leadership roles in their parishes, and it generally contrasts with their predecessors' definition. The women see themselves as copastors in the parish, and this is manifested in the way they work together with their parishioners on a daily basis. Evidence for this generalization was found in field notes and interviews.

AVAILABILITY

A key ingredient for collaborative leadership requires that the leader be available to his or her coworkers. In every parish visited, the previous pastor had been a priest, and in fifteen of the twenty parishes these priests were resident pastors (that is, they lived in the rectory or parish house) prior to the woman's appointment. Although the priests had lived in the parish house, and supposedly were available to practice collaborative leadership, this was seldom the actuality. In most cases availability to the parishioners was not possible because the priests had other duties outside the parish: some worked full-time in a diocesan office, others served another parish or two in addition to their own.

By contrast, none of the women pastors had other full-time jobs, yet five of them were in charge of a second church, and five were sharing parenting responsibilities because of children living at home. In general, however, their parishioners who typically had limited access to the previous pastors found that their pastor was more available to them. One parishioner expressed it this way:

> She is more visible than he [the former pastor] was. Again, he had two parishes, plus he was very active in AIDS education, and working with people with AIDS. And I think that was part of the reason he requested some help here because we hardly ever saw him. We would see him on Sunday and Saturday night for the services, and that was pretty much all we'd ever see him. Maybe that's part of the reason this transition went so well, too, because all of a sudden we have someone a lot more accessible than Father [the former pastor] was.

LINKAGES

Another key ingredient for collaborative leadership is that the leader have connections or linkages to the community. Creating and maintaining such linkages requires a certain amount of accessibility to the leader. Half of the women pastors I visited were living in the parish house. Five of the parishes had no parish house, and three of the rectories were too small for a family. In general, the married women remained in their own homes situated in the parish, and the nuns and the single lay-woman lived in the parish house. Exceptions to this were the married couple recruited from outside the parish who lived in the parish house, and three nuns who lived in rental units reasonably close to the church.

One of the women described her role with regard to the linkages with the community as a "hub." When someone asked her how she saw her role in the parish, she told me that she answered in this way:

> I see myself as the hub. I am connected to all these committees and I let everybody know what is going on. I am the one who is keeping everybody connected to each other.

Keeping everyone connected means that she must be accepted by all segments of the parish so that she can bridge them and thus begin to form the linkages between and among her parishioners. One of the male parishioners attested to this:

> In any community, the more people you have—we are still very small—but you have diversity. We have a conservative segment, and a very liberal segment, a charismatic segment, and [the woman pastor] is one of the few individuals in our parish group who is respected by all segments. So she has the ability to pull it all together.

Another parishioner described the segments in social class terms in the following way:

> In a rural area especially, if you spend too much time with—I want to use the word cliques—there are people who tend to find it very important socially to be active in the church, and I believe a lot of time spent with those people can narrow your social focus to that group of people and I think it's more damaging. Sister has tried to not have that occur. So she's focusing on all the social-economic aspects of the parish.

After I had attended a coffee and donut reception following Sunday Mass in the church basement, the married woman pastor who had been a parishioner there before her appointment explained to me that the occupants of each of the tables represented various cliques in the parish. She said that she systematically moved from table to table each week, so as not to be seen as favoring one clique over another.

However, some of the women I visited were more available to their parishioners than others, and thus better able to form linkages. As mentioned above, one-fourth of the women pastors interviewed were administering another parish or mission as well as their own, which lessened their accessibility. There was one case, in fact, where she was administering two mission churches in addition to her own parish.

Because I had made it a practice to follow each of the women pastors as they performed their various duties, I was exhausted after my visit to the last mentioned parish. On that occasion I traveled with her for many miles over winding roads to the three churches, attended three Masses, a baptism where she preached and assisted the priest, a baptismal party following the ceremony, and a parish potluck dinner.

Since women like her are "on the road" so much, their parishioners likewise have less access to her than they would if her sole responsibility was one parish. She is, of course, aware of that, and tries to "make up" for it by visiting the parishioners in their homes, because she values the linkages with them. As she explained it to me, she always accepted any invitations from parishioners to visit their homes if she could do so, because she got to know them better. As she put it, "People are open to visits; in fact they are thrilled to have someone visit their homes."

This outreach orientation, the practice of visiting parishioners' homes, was very prevalent in the parishes I visited. It was not only appreciated, but it was typically a "first" for most parishioners. In fact, many of them testified that her visit marked the first time a leader of the church had ever come to their homes.

Women pastors reciprocally valued their connections with the parishioners. One of them spoke very warmly about her linkages with the parishioners, and particularly about how her parishioners included her in their lives. For example, she said,

> A lot of the young women were having a housewarming across the street and they'll call and say, "We're having a housewarming. Come on over." I can't imagine they would have called a priest. Even the guys wouldn't have said, "Hey,

Father, come hunting with us." So you are included a lot in their life.

Another instrument they use to create linkages with the parishioners is the Sunday bulletin. In contrast to the formal style of most church bulletins, the ones I collected in my visits to these parishes are both more creative and more personal. Not only is the name of each parishioner with weekly liturgical duties listed and help solicited for projects in the future, but parishioners are also thanked by name for their work on previous church activities. The artistic talent of some of these women also makes reading their bulletins a more pleasant experience. Due to lack of secretarial help, about half of the women I interviewed told me that they typed the bulletins themselves.

Another means of communication and linkage to the parishioners was mentioned by a woman pastor:

> I inform them [parish committees] of every single thing that's going on so that they always know they are on the inside, and somehow just knowing what's going on helps them to believe they are making a decision about it, too. And they are. So I think communication is just very important that way.

LAY IDENTITY

Besides their greater accessibility, and the priority they place on making connections with their parishioners, there are other reasons why women tend to evidence collaborative leadership, rather than the hierarchical leadership style of their predecessors. They identify very strongly with the parishioners who, like themselves, are laity. This is in contrast to their predecessors, most of whom perceived themselves as occupying a special status, apart from and well above the laity.

We have to keep in mind that these women were not prepared for the the role of pastor in the same way as were their predecessors. In contrast to their predecessors, they were not exposed to the clerical socialization process where they learned the appropriate behavior expected of priest-pastors. Although over half of the women have master's degrees in theology, they did not earn their degrees in classrooms solely occupied by clergy or clerical aspirants, as did many of their predecessors.

The parishioners whom I interviewed not only recognized but tended to accept this hierarchical type of leadership of the priest when he was their pastor. As one female parishioner whose parish has had a lay pastor for two years explained,

> I didn't always feel like a lay person or a deacon could replace a priest because we always used to put priests up on a pedestal. And they were really special and nobody could fill their shoes. But my thinking has changed over the past few years.

Likewise, a male parishioner whose parish had a woman pastor for three years described how she truly labored together with the parishioners:

> [She] is not afraid to get out and minister, to get out and work at things and not sit back and give orders to somebody else to do the work. [She] is not afraid to pitch in, will go anywhere, anytime, for a meeting, to give a class, anything that needs to be done, to get a program going. [She] will devote her time and energy to it. She makes sure it's done; she doesn't just drop the ball. [She] does a good job of that, and that's something we didn't have before. Priests we have had don't take the initiative. They put themselves on a pedestal and let somebody else do the work. Right now we are getting more total community effort than we ever have because she is so active. We have had priests who would sit in this rectory while classes were going on next door and go for months without showing up.

In another parish, with four years of experience with a woman pastor, a parishioner stated:

> I think they [the parishioners] give her more than they did to the priests because previously, as I mentioned, the priests were more aloof, and there is a one-to-one thing going on here. We have a closer relationship [with the woman pastor], I think.

This does not mean, however, that all priests exercise leadership like the predecessors of the woman pastors in my study. Priests in various parts of the country, considered "good pastors" by their parishioners, tend to emphasize collaboration rather than authoritarianism. However, we should keep in mind that most of the parishes I visited were small isolated rural parishes, not the kind of parish that tends to get the "cream of the crop" for pastors. Some of these parishes, in fact, were viewed as the "last choice" by the priests of the diocese, and so were the first to lose a resident priest when the diocese felt the effects of the clergy shortage.

One of the parishioners, who was describing the problems the parish council had with the previous pastor, put it this way:

> It was just the priest who was here. He was very sick, became very sick mentally. He was here for [a number of] years, and the pressure was always there because we were always a small parish. We always had to respect the priest, and he had the run of the mill and we couldn't say anything. We had no say. We had a council in name only.

A male parishioner in another parish said,

> We had a priest who wanted to do everything and the parish, as a whole, became crippled, I think. And we are just learning that we can walk. The lay people are real good at fundraising and teaching for CCD, but I think we forget that we can minister to each other.

A female parishioner from the same parish said,

> [The lay pastor] is very good at delegating authority and letting people then do [the job]. That was a problem that Father [the previous pastor] had. He would ask for sharing of responsibility but didn't delegate to a point where a person would really feel they were fully sharing it, so they would sort of draw back and then the job wouldn't get done.

On one of my parish visits I observed a ceremony that exemplifies the delegating of authority to parishioners. At the end of Sunday Mass, the priest announced that the woman pastor would give some announcements and commission a eucharistic minister. The pastor then proceeded up the aisle, and went to the lectern. After making a few announcements, she called a parishioner by name to come up to the sanctuary, and explained that this woman, as a representative of the parish, would be taking Communion to parishioners in a convalescent home. The pastor then solemnly commissioned her to do so, and symbolically placed her hand on the woman's head as she made the invocation.

Another point to keep in mind is how these women were recruited to their present position, because it has a bearing on their leadership style. Although all of them were ultimately appointed by the bishop, in only a fourth of the cases was the recruitment initiated by the bishop or another diocesan official. Over half were recruited by the parishioners themselves or by a local priest. Three of the women applied for the job, and in one case it was the woman's religious community who asked the bishop to appoint one of their members. Because of the way they were recruited, many of these women have a strong sense of loyalty to the parishioners, and tend to see themselves as sharing their leadership with them.

The importance of their identity as laity is especially true for the seven women who were active in the parish as parishioners themselves before the appointment, and the three women who had worked in the parish as parish associates for a number of years prior to the appointment. As I mentioned in chapter 2, in these ten parishes the person chosen for the leadership role emerged from the parish itself. Although officially appointed by the bishop, in the last analysis she was chosen as head of the parish by the parishioners themselves, who knew her, trusted her, and recognized her leadership abilities.

Parishioners described some rather dramatic instances when the bishop or his representative came to meet with the parish council to explain why there would no longer be a resident priest assigned to the parish, and to discuss the situation. The alternatives he proposed included the following: closing the parish, advertising nationally for a priest to fill the position, recruiting a priest from a foreign country like India or the Phillipines, finding a male deacon, or recruiting a nonordained lay person. Invariably the parish council members, who recognized the quality of leadership that she had already exercised in the community, told the bishop, "We want _____," and pointed her out.

In one diocese the bishop sent a representative from the chancery office to meet with the parish council and to discuss the possibilities of a pastoral team made up of parishioners with one person as their leader. The council members pointed to one of the women on the council and said, "She will be that person for us, because she's our spokesperson."

One of the women chosen by her parishioners, who is deeply loved and respected by them, explained her perspective on leadership:

> Leadership is listening to parishioner's initiatives. A leader listens and then articulates the needs and direction of the community, and finds ways to name it and to facilitate it. The most valuable thing I think anybody could have who would find themselves in this position [as pastor] would be to maintain their sense of deep respect for all of the people that you work with and not think that you are in a position of authority over them; that's not what being a parish leader is about.

By contrast, another women pastor who likewise emerged from among the parishioners did not find it easy to exercise a collaborative leadership style. She explained that her previous experience as a business administrator for several years "got in her way" at times. As she explained it,

> I was a real tough Sarge; it was my way or no way. And it got done and it was right. But you can't work that way in the church. So I really had to turn around and really learn collaboration. I find it frustrating because I can get things done and get them done in a hurry, and when I give it to a committee, six months later they are still fighting about it. But my whole style of leadership has changed from the business world, very consciously.

The tendency to take over and do it herself when a project was limping along was simply not an option for most of the women I visited. These women were very talented, and could easily have taken over a myriad of additional jobs in the parish, like training teachers and teaching in the religious education programs; running the liturgy program, including directing the choir and playing the organ; running the youth programs, etc. Indeed, the list of their possible contributions, in addition to their pastoral duties, is almost endless. The temptation to take on some of this additional work is more acute during the first year of their pastoral experience, when they were "groping their way," and learning how to keep a parish running. But the reality is that, short of acquiring the miraculous power of bilocation, they simply don't have the time to take on these extra tasks. In fact, only about half of them consistently take a day off, which is provided in their contracts.

After at least one year's experience in the position, however, the women pastors learned not to give in to the temptation to take over, because of the long-run implications, certainly including a possible burnout for them. How did they accomplish this?

STRATEGIES: LETTING GO AND INCLUSION

Their chief strategy could be described as "letting go," or "forgetting." This simply means that they consciously "forgot" that they had talents like playing the organ, leading the choir, running youth programs, etc. Indeed, some said they had to keep reminding themselves that these talents were forgotten! But, as one put it, "It takes time and it takes letting go, and it takes letting people fumble around."

One of the rewards of letting go that was mentioned by many was "watching people grow." Here is an example:

> Sometimes I have a hard time letting go of things and I have to be real careful of that. I had done the liturgy and process for an Evening of Prayer for three years. I enjoy doing that. This last spring [one of the parishioners] asked me if she could do it, and I had an awful time letting go of that, but I said, "Yes." And I watched her put together something that was better than I would have done because she took more time at it, and it was a new experience for her and she wasn't relying on things that had worked in the past. She put together something that was better than I would have done. And I sat back and said, "Okay."

What they found was that parishioners were more willing to be active participants, and even to "fumble around" when the agenda was theirs, not the pastor's. One of the parishioners described a "listening session" conducted by the lay pastor soon after her arrival, where the parishioners were asked what they wanted to see done and how they wanted their parish to grow. One of the results of the listening session was the formation of a liturgy commission headed by and composed of parishioners, who then continued the listening process in this way:

> One of the first things we did as a commission was put a survey out to the people and try to get a feel of specifically what things in the liturgy they wanted to see changed, or how they feel about this or what made them feel good, or what they didn't like. So that's what our goal is, to try to make the Sunday Mass and special liturgies more meaningful.

We can expect a more collaborative style of leadership in parishes where the leadership of the women emerged from the parish itself because she is not an unknown entity, a stranger who was thrust upon them by the bishop. She has already earned the trust and esteem of the parishioners; in a real sense she was their candidate. In none of the parishes had the previous [priest] pastor ever been a member of the parish prior to his appointment. One of the predecessors had served as an associate pastor earlier in his priestly career, but his appointment came directly from the bishop; the parishioners had no say in the matter. In fact, most current diocesan norms [written and unwritten] in this country tend to prohibit or at least discourage the assignment of priests to their own family parishes.

One can only speculate about the ultimate advantages and disadvantages of appointing someone to this position who is already a member of the parish or who has worked in the parish previously. That it was an advantage for the women in my study may be a function of the parishioners' anxiety about the survival of their parish. All of these parishes suffer this anxiety. The very fact that they have been designated for alternate staffing and do not have a resident priest places the parish in a precarious state.

Therefore, the parishioners in these "priestless parishes" are ripe for a strategy of inclusion. Reaching out to the parishioners and attempting to include them in the business of keeping the parish operating has every chance of success in a situation like this one. It is a basic sociological tenet that a group threatened by an outside force tends to experience an increase of solidarity, and to stand together as they struggle for their survival.[2] The women who were parishioner-pastors are not newcomers to the threatened parish. It follows, then, that cooperation is not difficult to come by, as the following statement attests: "We worked it out. We said, 'We are all in this boat together. We either go down or stay afloat.'"

Another parishioner in a parish with an "insider" pastor said,

> It's hard to say no to [her] because people respect her and you want to help her. And she just has a way of asking you that puts you at ease. It's not in a demanding sort of way at all. She always *asks,* never says, "Do this."

The acceptance by the parishioners was not automatic, however. One of the women, who had grown up in a neighboring parish, described an incident that happened on the occasion when a representative from the bishop's office came to announce her appointment as head of the parish.

> Then [the bishop's representative] came and celebrated all the Masses and told the people what was happening and introduced me at the Masses. That was an interesting experience because a lot of the people didn't know me. I was sitting behind a couple of women who were sitting there saying, "No way, no way in the world will I accept a woman in charge. No way." Out loud, during the homily. The reaction was that strong.

When the woman pastor was asked to stand, she said that the women sitting in front of her "would have liked to have crawled under their seats." However, both of them eventually became strong supporters of the parish, because she always greeted them by name and took Communion to them when they were sick. As she explained, "After that I could do no wrong." Again, the strong belief in making linkages by reaching out to parishioners paid off.

In parishes where the woman pastor was not an "insider," there were similar sentiments voiced by parishioners regarding the way they were enlisted to help in the running of the parish. Here are three examples:

> She's got a certain way about doing it. It is the way she comes on. She is very, very pleasant and she is the type of person that you want to help because you know she is doing so much within the parish. So you feel, "I am part of this parish; I want to take some of the load off of her." And it is very hard to say no to [her]. That is the bottom line.

We have far more leadership and caring, nurturing, bringing out of talent than we have ever had here. [She] is always
involved and always present, and I have worked with so many
priests who don't care. [She] is involved in the planning and
cares.

Personal contact, a lot of personal contact, and of course,
the usual, the blurb in the bulletin and having other people to
spread the word around and ask other parishioners if they
would be involved. She has a way of knowing what an individual's talents are and calling them forth.

When I asked the women pastors how they went about getting the parishioners involved, most of them replied that they
did it on an individual basis as well as on a group basis, asking
people in general to help, but then contacting people directly
and suggesting some specific project to them. Most of the time
they received positive responses, as this pastor indicates:

I ask more of them. They weren't asked to do these things [by
the priest]. They respond. Sometimes it scares me because
some of them will say to me, "Sister, I can't say no to you. I
don't want to do it but I can't say no to you." They said that
with a little bit of fear, too, that "if I don't do it she might leave
and then we won't have a parish." But I also think they do it
out of affection.

One of the women pastors elaborated on the consequences
of the inclusion strategy.

This is quite a breakthrough for people who formerly had little
say in parish direction or planning. In this and other rural
areas, the priest-pastor frequently acted as the parish council,
the bus driver, the school superintendent, the choir director,
and even the athletic coach. The one way that people knew to
do something was "Father's way," or "the way we always did
it." Now we are discovering better ways of meeting today's
needs by drawing on all the personal insight and initiative
available to us.

Women pastors tend to be very sensitive about the problem
of usurping the parishioners' authority, even in seemingly small
ways. For instance, the parishioners in one parish had experienced a period of nine months without a resident pastor before
her arrival, and they had taken over a variety of duties to keep

the church activities going. She explained one of her efforts to continue the empowerment of the parishioners.

> When I came, there was a group of women in the parish that met every morning for a Communion service and when the deacon left nine months before he said to them, "You can still continue to meet even though I am not going to be there." And he gave them a missalette[3] and he showed them which prayers to read and they simply carried on in a real simple way. They just simply read the prayers, found the reading, read the reading and had Communion. So when I arrived they assumed that I would just take over and that they would go back to their places. And I didn't. I said, "Oh, this is the future. We'll just take turns."

She then continued, revealing her commitment to training for lay leadership:

> But then I knew that I wanted to help them develop that presiding skill, because they weren't doing it well, and sometimes they weren't even finding the readings for the day. But now we have a beautiful, prayerful sharing of the Scriptures every morning. They never talked about the Scriptures before. They just read them and then they went on. Now they sit right down and we share and it's real different. So I am glad that I didn't just take over. I could have.

Another example of the careful attention to the problem of usurping parishioner's rights was presented by a parishioner who described the lengths his pastor went to in order to bring parishioners into a renovation process.

> She's currently involved in renovating the church. We've done an awful lot with the inside of the church, but she really tried very hard to meet the wants of the people. She had an idea of how she wanted the church to be laid out, but rather than just go ahead with that she talked to several people that were very active in the church, and asked for their suggestions. And we came up, in the end, with five possibilities.

He then continued to describe the process:

> So what we did is we rearranged the church in those five different ways. Each week we would come to Mass and the church would be laid out in a different fashion. The seats were

all unbolted from the floor so they were adjustable. But Sister did it over a period of time and she asked for input from the people. As each step went by, she kept saying, "Is this the way you like it? Keep in mind this because next week we're going to try something different." And then, in the end, after five weeks of having things rearranged and having people totally confused, she asked for the consensus of opinion as to which was the most effective way. So even for something as small as laying out the church, it wasn't her rule.

CONSEQUENCES OF COLLABORATIVE LEADERSHIP

Two of the most apparent consequences of the collaborative leadership exercised by these women were increased participation of the parishioners and a growing spirit of solidarity within the parish. The first, parishioner participation, could be quantified by increased numbers of committees and active committee members, an increase in church attendance, and in contributions to the Sunday collection. The contributions were usually reported in the Sunday bulletin, and a perusal of these revealed that there was, in general, an increase in contributions, particularly after her first year as pastor. One of the women pastors attributed the increase in contributions to the inclusion process. She said,

> When I came the contributions increased quite a bit, actually. Now it has continued to be on a pretty stable level. And the people have told me they are beginning to see where some of their money is going. They liked the fact that I was putting a little more into education. It came in when they saw where the money was going.

Many of the parishioners I interviewed attested to the fact that more families had joined the parish, and attendance at other parish activities had increased. My examination of parish attendance records corroborated the parishioners' perceptions. Summing it up, a parishioner said, "There are definitely more people at Mass now, more people at everything and more people doing things."

In a similar vein, parishioners told me that there were people in the parish who had not been involved for twenty years prior to the arrival of their woman pastor, but who were now actively working on parish committees. As one parishioner put it, "The same old people did everything until she came."

The second consequence of collaborative leadership—a growing spirit of community—is more elusive, and difficult to quantify. A careful reading of the parish bulletins prepared by the women pastors indicates how they foster a feeling of "we-ness" in the parish. Terms like "our church" and "our parish" are used over and over again. What I observed in the friendliness of the atmosphere at various parish functions, the warm greetings to each other on arriving and leaving the church, and the words used by parishioners to describe their solidarity all attested to this phenomenon. Time and time again, both in the interviews and in casual conversation, parishioners would refer to the parish in the first person plural.

An example of the feeling of we-ness comes from one of the poorest parishes I visited. One Saturday afternoon I observed a female parishioner who was helping to clean the interior of the church. She was not only dusting the furniture and vacuuming the floor, but she was also sweeping down the walls of the church, as far as she could reach. When I complimented her for her thoroughness, she said that she was pleased to participate in keeping "our church" clean, and proudly introduced me to to her son who was also a member of the cleaning crew.

In another parish on a Saturday morning, several male parishioners arrived at 8:30 to work with steel brushes on the exterior of the church, preparing it for a new stain job. About the same time a few of the women arrived to begin preparing strawberry shortcake as a treat for the workers. I observed the camaraderie that existed among the workers on the ladders and on the roof as well as in the kitchen. Later as I sat among them, enjoying the strawberry shortcake and listening to their conversations, I heard the words "we" and "our" whenever they referred to the church or to parish activities.

One of the parishioners described his sense of solidarity with his parish this way:

> I was baptized here, confirmed here. All my kids have been baptized and confirmed here. My Dad is also buried in that cemetery. All my grandparents and aunts and uncles are buried down there, also. My daughter is buried there. So I

have a real tie to that church, and my feelings for that church—I mean, if it closes it is going to be very hard, very troublesome for me to accept. I have been on the parish council now, my second term. I am treasurer of the cemetery committee, and I just love helping that church, my church.

Another manifestation of the spirit of parish solidarity that I observed occurred after Sunday Mass, when the parishioners congregated outside the church or in the basement drinking coffee together, a recent phenomenon at some of the parishes I visited. Parishioners reported that prior to the arrival of the woman pastor, people usually went directly home after church services, but that now they typically hang around and visit with each other before leaving. The "hanging around" could last anywhere from fifteen minutes to an hour, and it tended to be more prolonged when it included donuts and coffee. It may be, in part, a function of their location in isolated rural areas, and the distances some of them must drive in order to participate in parish activities, but these parishioners seemed genuinely glad to see each other, and enjoyed "catching up" on each other on these occasions.

One of the pastors talked about her bishop's reaction to the leadership style of women pastors:

He [the bishop] said that what he sees in the parishes where there are pastoral administrators [lay pastors], is a real sense of community and a special something that he can't always identify that he sees there that he doesn't see in the other parishes. And I am not saying those parishes aren't good, but he can see something distinctive about the leadership of the women as pastoral administrators, and community was the thing.

A priest whom I interviewed also attested to the spirit of community in a parish headed by a woman. He said,

I guess I feel, in a sense, there is a loss for the people here without a resident priest, just because I think the very nature of priesthood has something basic to do with Catholic life and they don't have that. But on a more personal level, in terms of what I see happening here, she's been the best thing that's happened to this parish in twenty years because she has been able to pull the community together and get them working. I feel an incredible sense of community here that she, in her very humble kind of way, has been able to do. People have accepted her as a leader and I really don't feel the parish is missing anything.

A female parishioner from the same parish echoed his sentiments when she said,

> We were losing parishioners and losing the feel of community. It didn't have the closeness it had before. The priest coming in from St. _____ was doing a very good job, but it was just that he didn't have the time to dedicate to all of the extracurricular activities that we did have. This is a community where the church is the central location because there is nothing else. So we would come to church activities that would build this community. We don't have a store or central post office or town, not even a meeting place. Our meeting place is here at the church. And we were losing that.

My last example of increased solidarity as a consequence of collaborative leadership is one that emerged from what I observed when I accompanied a woman pastor on her visit to the home of a parishioner with a terminal case of cancer. Although very weak, and scarcely able to speak, the woman's face lighted up when her pastor asked her if she was remembering to take her medicine. The pastor explained that the woman who was ill had difficulty remembering to set her alarm clock, so a team of parishioners volunteered to take turns phoning her at various points of the day, including at two and four in the morning, to remind her that it was medicine time. Though her words were barely audible, it was obvious that this woman was expressing her appreciation for the efforts of the parishioners on her behalf, and was deeply touched by the expressions of their commitment to her.

In summing up the different leadership style of women pastors, it is clear that although the road to collaborative leadership is not always smooth and can be very circuitous and time consuming, it is the direction they are taking. Clearly some women pastors have moved further along in their collaborative efforts than others, but I found that all of them are clearly oriented to that type of leadership style. In fact, a female parishioner labeled collaborative leadership as a "movement" in the right direction. She said,

I don't see this whole movement as something negative. I see
it as something that's really positive because I think the Church
is going back to what it was very, very early when it was
much more people-oriented, and much less run by a hierarchy. I like seeing control and responsibility being shifted to the
laity. I don't think we would ever be getting this if we did not
have a priest shortage.... That's a new idea for a lot of people,
to have this much involvement in running your church, in
deciding your liturgy, and still remaining Catholic, true to the
faith, I think is healthy. I think our faith is becoming ours
rather than belonging to a priest.

What this parishioner is alluding to is the movement toward a
restructuring of authority in the parish, from a hierarchical to a circular relationship between parishioner and pastor. This type of
parish restructuring, both a cause and a consequence of the collaborative direction these nonordained pastors are taking as leaders of the parish, is the topic I will discuss in the next chapter.

•5•

Parish Restructuring

When Pope John XXIII convened the Second Vatican Council in 1962, he made it clear that he wanted the Church to move in new directions. He stressed two changes in particular. First, he underlined the importance of *aggiornamento,* an updating or modernization process, which he often described as "opening the windows of the Church to the outside world," thus signaling an end to isolationism. For instance, when he publicly embraced a prominent rabbi, and referred to him as "Joseph, my brother," Pope John was acting out his belief in *aggiornamento.* This symbolic moment was an impetus for the ecumenical thrust of Vatican II. Although the ecumenical movement has experienced a series of reversals in the past twenty-five years, that new direction taken by the Catholic church received international press coverage, and one could argue that the President of the Soviet Union, Mikhail Gorbachev, was borrowing from Pope John's *aggiornamento* when he launched his *glasnost* program.

The second direction proposed by Pope John XXIII, and the one most relevant to the topic of this chapter, which he labeled coresponsibility, also bears some resemblance to Gorbachev's second key concept, *perestroika.* Both coresponsibility and *perestroika* represent proposals for a serious restructuring of institutions in order to bring about internal changes. In the case of the Catholic church, coresponsibility means that there will be significant changes in the relationships between clergy and laity. Without a change in ideology regarding the meaning of the church, that is, an ecclesiological redefinition, coresponsibility would not be possible.

A REDEFINITION OF CHURCH

The Vatican Council's definition of the church simply as the "people of God" required a radical change in thinking for both clergy and laity, from "we-they" to "us." It meant that the laity were no longer "quasicitizens" of the church, with the clergy alone retaining full citizenship. Inclusion of the laity gave them the right to participate in making decisions, in shaping policy, and in changing legislation, all of which had been seen as the prerogative of the clergy. One of the women who had been a parishioner in her parish for several years before her appointment as its pastor described how some changes in thinking came about as parishioners moved from quasi-citizenship to full citizenship in her parish:

> We had a group of parishioners that studied some of the documents on Vatican II that said the people are the Church. That was a whole new experience to think of yourselves as church because we always knew that the priests and nuns were the church and the rest of you were just there. So we went through a number of months of formation forming the parish council and identifying, and beginning to say "we are the Church."

We can expect that the process of moving from a hierarchical or pyramidal structure to a circular one will not be smooth, especially in a church that has a long history of hierarchy with clergy on the top and laity on the bottom. As one woman pastor put it, "The laity as laity have been peasants." The Soviet Union's experience has thus far illustrated that the restructuring process is fraught with difficulties, not the least of which is persuading the people of the value of *perestroika,* so that they will be willing to do their part toward moving their society in this new direction.

It may be that a lay pastor will be more effective in restructuring the parish than a priest, because a priest's presence may intimidate parishioners and inhibit their adoption of a new way of thinking about the church. A male parishioner who had four years of experience with a woman as the leader of his parish put it this way:

I feel part of the church now. I didn't feel part of the church before. It was the priest. He did everything; he did all the thinking. Now the responsibility has been sent down to us and in our parish it is working great. I think it's the best thing that ever happened here. I am encouraged. I love it. It's our church.

For the average Catholic, whether clergy or laity, thinking of the Church as the people of God requires a radical change in consciousness. It means changing the meaning of church from an institution owned and operated by the pope, bishops, and clergy to an awareness that we—that is, clergy and laity alike— are the church; in short, a belief personified in the quote above that it's "our church," not "theirs." The change in thinking then leads to relationships that are egalitarian, nonhierarchical, and mutually supportive.

We cannot expect a more active participation on the part of the laity without this change in thinking, because the pre-Vatican II definition of church placed the laity in a predominantly passive position, much like that of an audience during a theatrical performance. The priest-pastor was often depicted as a "one-man band," who did everything of significance in the parish, especially the thinking and decision making, and who shared no leadership with the laity, as the male parishioner attests in the above quote. The women pastors whom I observed, on the other hand, tended to be more like the conductor of an orchestra, who oversees all of the activity in the parish, but calls forth the talents of the parishioners who then willingly cooperate in taking on the responsibility for running the parish. In short, the laity "make the music," while the woman pastor orchestrates it.[1]

PARISHIONERS AS COPASTORS

This restructuring of the parish places the laity on stage as the principle actors in the performance, rather than in the audience or backstage. Because they are sharing in the leadership of the parish, the parishioners are more like copastors since they share in the decision making and in the activities that were formerly reserved to the priest. The dramaturgical concepts of frontstage and backstage regions in a performance are relevant here.[2] One could argue that the traditional stance of the priest-pastor was like an actor performing in the frontstage region, where he defined the situation for those observing his performance by the use of "expressive equipment," like his Roman collar, vestments worn during liturgical ceremonies, and his general demeanor including posture, facial expressions and body gestures, all of which enabled him to place himself on a level above his parishioners. In this hierarchical situation the majority of the parishioners are silent and passive members of the audience; a few are backstage assisting the main actor [priest] to succeed in his performance as the person solely in charge of the parish: the housekeeper, secretary, altar servers, janitor, etc.

By contrast, women pastors do not place themselves above the parishioners, and tend to find ways to eradicate, or at least to decrease, clerical privilege and status, and to reaffirm their positions as members of the laity. As one of them said,

> There are different ways of leading, and I would never want to see any one person taking over the role. Some people have called me "Pastor," and I always say, "No, I am not the pastor. We are all pastor together."

Some of the women pastors make the point of copastoring symbolically by sitting in the pews with the congregation during Mass, so that they are seen as an equal among equals. They also place laity with leadership responsibilities [like the lectors, eucharistic ministers, and song leaders] in the sanctuary with the priest, thus forcing the priest to "share the limelight," as it were, with other frontstage performers.

One woman pastor made this comparison:

> I don't think that the priest I am working with has the same vision of empowerment of lay people. He can say all the right words, but at the gut level he doesn't allow it to happen.

One could argue that the reason the vision cannot be shared is that the two principal "viewers" are standing in different positions. The priest is looking on from above, as it were, from his privileged position as clergy. He was once a layperson, but for most priests that was a long time ago, in the days of his youth. Understandably a priest would find it hard to remember how it felt to be a layman, and what the church looked like from that vantage point.

On the other hand, the women pastors, nuns and married women alike, have always been laypersons, even though they are temporarily in charge of a parish. They continue to be reminded of their limited empowerment as they struggle to perform a job without the proper credentials. Therefore, their vision of the empowerment of lay people tends to be crystal clear, as is evidenced in the following statement from a sister who had been pastoring for over five years:

> In my heart I consider myself laity, and the more enabled I can move this [parish], not only for women but for laity.... The other kind of hierarchical church is gradually going to become extinct, and then we will have the laity more enabled and ready.
>
> And another thing is because I am not in a class, in a sense, like a priest would be, I see where I can get in there and be part of that change without a class system attached to me. Even if there was ordination [for women], if that would ever come to be, I am sure I don't want it to be what it is. So I question ordination as such, because one of my firm beliefs is we could ordain women who would be doing the same things as men, but living in female bodies, and then we would still have the hierarchical [structure]. And that isn't the ordination that I'm looking toward. I am looking toward a more circular ordination that puts together the gifts of all people.

Parish restructuring has not been a smooth process. It requires power sharing, often a painful experience, because those in power are not in a hurry to give it up, and parishioners may require much persuasion to take on parish responsibilities. Thus the attitude of the "one in charge," the pastor, who proposes the restructuring in the first place, is the key to the success or failure of parish restructuring.

POWER SHARING

One of the first signs of parish restructuring is evident as one enters the door of the church. There, inside the entrance is a bulletin board filled with information about upcoming events and other announcements, but always in a prominent place are the names of parishioners who comprise the numerous parish committees. Over fifty percent of parishioners in most of these parishes are active members of a committee, and some estimates of parishioner participation were as high as eighty or ninety percent. As one parishioner described it, "There are some members in this parish who were inactive for over twenty years until she came along and recruited them." These committees are chaired and run by parishioners who are totally "in charge." The woman pastor oversees them, but rarely overrides their decisions.

Some dioceses provide guidelines for lay leadership. For example one such guideline states that all laity should be encouraged to participate in some sort of service to the church. It further instructs the pastor to join with the pastoral council and staff to discern the gifts of leadership among the laity and to facilitate this leadership by providing educational programs and training sessions. Thus, the promotion of lay leadership may not be initiated by the woman pastor in some cases, but she is typically very diligent in pursuing the movement towards lay participation.

This is accomplished in a variety of ways, but most of the women pastors talk to people individually about their participation. Their appeal to the parishioners tends to be very effective, because of the their common bond as members of the laity. One of the women pointed to her preaching as a source of recruitment:

> When I preach I always come back to how do we minister in the parish and what are some of the needs. It is so automatic that I don't realize I am doing it until I reread it and see what I am doing. Everything that I do encourages people to do something.

Another tool, which many of the women utilize, is a yearly sign-up sheet that is distributed to every parishioner. One woman describes her method in this way:

> Every year at our stewardship drive before we talk about money we talk about time and talent. And we ask people to fill out a Time and Talent sheet that has so many different things on it that there is something everybody can commit to, including praying for the needs of the parish. So we invite people to do something, even if it is something like doing nothing but saying an "Our Father" once a day at home. And we don't have very many who only accept that [responsibility].

Another way to encourage participation is to recognize the parishioners who are active. Most of the parish bulletins that are distributed each week listed all of the members of the parish committees and the names of those who had specific duties for the current week. But some women pastors found additional ways to acknowledge parishioner participation. For instance, as mentioned earlier, during the announcements made before the beginning of the Sunday Mass, one woman pastor read the name of each parishioner who was performing a duty during the ceremony. Although the names of these parishioners were listed on the bulletin board, this additional recognition in the form of a public act of gratitude was impressive, and was well received by the congregation.

A final example of parishioner encouragement comes from a parish that initiated an "Appreciation Day." As the pastor described it,

> Three years ago at the parish council meeting I said, "Now we are going to have the picnic again and I am wondering if it might be a good time to express our gratitude to each other because we've really developed over the past year and a half" [because that's how long I had been there]. "We need to recognize people." So the parish council really picked up on that and we decided that we would combine recognition and appreciation with the picnic. And at that time I made out certificates for every single person and [distributed] them, and we got balloons and had a big sign made and had the picnic outside.

The parish council, composed of elected parishioners, is the key group for parish decision making. Important decisions from other committees are usually filtered through the parish council before any action is taken. Although the woman pastor typically attends all meetings of the parish council, she is usually on an equal footing with them with regard to voting, and if she has an override vote she seldom uses it. The priest who serves as sacramental minister does not attend the parish council meetings in most of the parishes I visited. In one parish where he did attend, a parishioner explained his role:

> He is usually at our parish council meetings. He is a real quiet man. He'll sit and listen, and then he may say something, or if he is asked for a comment, he'll comment on it. He doesn't try

to take over. This is very much our parish and he assists us.
He does not take a leadership role. He doesn't want one.

Parishioners and pastors alike described the decision making
in parish council meetings as a consensus situation. As a woman
pastor, a nun with many years of experience in rural ministry
explained it,

> It's really their agenda that we have to deal with. And so it is a
> gradual kind of process of getting them to own the agenda.
> The agenda includes many things now that were never talked
> about before.

In addition, the meetings of the parish council are typically
open to all members of the parish, so that any member of the
parish can attend if he or she wishes.

This is not to say that the decisions of the parish council are
accepted by the parishioners without question. Changes made
inside the parish church, like taking away the Communion rail
or moving the statues from the front to the back of the church,
are sometimes strongly resisted. One woman pastor described
the reaction of some parishioners who protested the proposal of
the parish council to remove the Communion rail:

> They would come to meetings of parish council to protest.
> There was a group of four or five who would come to several
> of the meetings that we had right after that. I didn't ever feel
> like I was doing it nor did I ever really feel like I was being
> attacked in that whole situation because it was not my plan; it
> was our plan. I never took ownership of it all by myself. I was
> not the only one who wanted to get rid of the communion rail.
> In fact, I almost tried to remain neutral by telling them that this
> was what Vatican II was really encouraging and trying to
> almost remain a neutral person, but educating them as to why
> we were going to be doing this. I would have comments like,
> "I am not going to come into the church again if you take out
> the Communion rail," or I would hear that through someone
> else. Very often I was not the one who was hearing this, but it
> would be said in downtown cafes and people would come
> back to me saying that this was being said.

The parishioners opposed to the removal of the altar rail
threatened to obstruct its removal, but when the truck arrived at

the church on the appointed day and time, no parishioners showed up to hinder the operation. Had they not been allowed to voice their criticisms throughout the decision-making process, the outcome might have been very different, because the removal of any of the treasured objects from the church can be a sensitive and painful issue, especially for elderly parishioners. Some of the priests interviewed, in fact, said that they wouldn't dream of bringing up the question of such changes in their church until several years after they had taken over as pastor.

What are the specific responsibilities taken on by parishioners in these parishes? I asked pastors and parishioners this question at each parish I visited, and was amazed at the length of the list presented to me. First of all, parishioners are in charge of scheduling classes, training teachers, and teaching in the religious education programs of the parish, which usually include both elementary and high school-aged children. Most parishes also have adult religious programs as well. Though the woman pastor oversees these programs, she seldom has the time to participate in any of the work of this committee, though she may occasionally teach a class in a teacher's absence.

Three-fourths of the parishes I visited were small, with less than two hundred families; the largest had 339 families registered in the parish. Not one of them owned a school building, so most of their religious education classes were held in the church basement. I watched the miraculous transformation of one church basement, where partitions were pulled out to transform it into eight classrooms in about ten minutes. The parishioner in charge of the religious education programs was very visible, answering parishioners' questions and supervising every aspect of the program.

I also observed one session of a confirmation class that was held in a parishioner's home one Sunday afternoon. Three parishioners took turns at teaching the groups of teenagers, while the woman pastor, other parents, and I sat quietly on the sidelines. However, during the last half hour, when she led them in a brief prayer session, it was evident that this pastor was no stranger to the children, for she called each one of them by name.

Another important committee, usually called the liturgy committee, assists in the choice of hymns for each Mass, trains and assigns parishioners as lectors, altar servers, participants in the offertory procession, readers of the prayers for the faithful, eucharistic ministers, and ushers. They usually set up the altar before Mass, and see that all of the musical equipment is in its proper place. This committee also has jurisdiction regarding any changes to be made inside the church itself, like placement of statues and pews.

The finance committee is in charge of parish accounts, the counting of collections made at Mass, making decisions about expenditures, and all other aspects of the parish budget. Although the financial report to the diocesan office is usually done by the pastor each year, most of the ingredients of that report are the responsibility of this committee. In some parishes the chair of this committee cosigns the checks with the pastor.

A married pastor's description of her parish finance committee is a good example of parish restructuring. She explained that the finance committee, made up of four parishioners and herself, arrives at the yearly budget by consensus. She explained:

> When I meet with them I give them an update of where we stand. And they see everything. This is something that they have been absolutely flabbergasted with. They never saw the books before; they never saw anything. They get an accounting of every last penny. They see everything that comes in, and how it is spent, and where we stand.

The outreach committee, often called St. Vincent de Paul, is responsible for collecting and distributing clothing, money, and food to those in need. Membership in the parish is seldom a requisite for aid from this group. Other outreach groups visit the sick and the elderly, and *ad hoc* groups are often formed in crisis situations. An incident I described earlier regarding the parishioners who came to the aid of a woman dying of cancer is a good example of one of these groups.

The altar society, usually composed of women parishioners, is in charge of cleaning the church, decorating the altar with flowers, and often sponsors cake sales and other events in order to raise money for church needs. In the previous chapter I described one of my observations of the work of a parish altar society on a Saturday afternoon when I talked to a woman who was sweeping down the walls of the church while her son was vacuuming the floor. She admitted that she took as much pride in this as in her own housecleaning, because it was "her church."

The building and maintenance committee is in charge of the maintenance and upkeep of all parish buildings and grounds. Since many of these parishes have very old buildings, this is a key committee. Half of the women interviewed were living in the parish house or rectory, and since I was their guest for the weekend I had a chance to witness some of their many "calls for help" as they phoned members of the maintenance committee when pipes burst or refrigerators needed repair. Help usually arrived within the hour, and the worker's typical attitude was that he was repairing "his" parish house. The grounds of these parishes were all well kept, but in one parish, the grounds were so unusually beautiful that I inquired about its upkeep. I was told that the groundskeeper was a retired person who took great pride in the maintenance of the lawns and flowers on the church property, spending many hours each week on this endeavor. Again, the superb groundskeeping was another indicator of parishioner ownership.

The young adult or youth committee organizes programs for the teenagers of the parish. This committee was defunct in many of the parishes, and this was a matter of concern to the pastor and parishioners, who realize that the future of the parish is in the hands of the younger generation. The enlistment of the youth in the running of the parish does not seem to be high on the current agenda in most parishes, however.

The Knights of Columbus, open only to men of the parish, was also defunct in most of the parishes. This is primarily a fraternal organization that provides male fellowship for members who desire it, and it also hosts fund-raising events for the parish.

All of the work on these committees is voluntary and unpaid. In two or three cases a small stipend was paid to the choir director and the director of religious education, but this was not usual. Almost all of these parishes are struggling financially, and the parishioners not only are well aware of their economic situation, but they also take an active part in the financial decisions of the parish.

As has been evident from the foregoing discussion, the

women in charge of these parishes have limited empowerment in a formal sense because they are not priests, and they cannot have the title of pastor because they are laity. They have been recruited to their position in the parish because of the clergy shortage, not because of a movement toward the inclusion of women in leadership positions, and this aspect of power sharing will be treated in a later chapter. Women pastors have a different view of the role of the parishioner than did their predecessors, as the following statement illustrates:

> I very much did not want to be a leader like some pastors I have seen, that they did everything they wanted to do and the people had no say about it. There were some things I saw would be an improvement or I really wanted to do but [decided] to be patient and wait until I knew that they agreed with it rather than just doing it, and then letting them say or not say what they felt about it afterwards.

One of the women pastors, who had been a member of the parish for several years before she was appointed to head the parish, described the consequences of her predecessor's stance thus:

> He didn't work well with people, was very demanding and argumentative, didn't want to be bothered half the time, saw no point in having people involved in things. The idea of eucharistic ministers was ridiculous, and all the things we had built up over the years. The unfortunate thing was he still wanted to be in a church of thirty years ago and we were at a point, as a parish, having established our parish council and over the years [had] come to see that we had to be the church here, because we would either have priests with bad health or no priests. So if the people didn't see to the life of the church and the activity and all the other things—if we didn't see to it, it wasn't going to happen. So we have developed a strong sense of involvement and ownership.

For the married women pastors, their prior experience as parishioners in the parish they were heading enabled them to encourage the emergence of a strong sense of community among the parishioners. They were leaders who had a history of sharing in the sufferings and joys of their parishioners.

FACILITATING FACTORS FOR LAY OWNERSHIP

As I see it, the following are the factors that facilitate the restructuring of parishes: (1) close identity of a pastor with lay parishioners; (2) previous membership in the parish (an "insider" pastor); (3) pressure felt by parishioners to help in the survival of the parish; and (4) the base community model. The first three factors were dealt with earlier in the previous chapter, so I begin with a discussion of the fourth factor, base communities.

Some of the nun pastors whom I interviewed had Third World experience, which was an important preparation for parish restructuring. In particular, four of them had participated in the development of basic ecclesial communities, often called base communities, as part of their parish work in Latin America. Base communities are small groups led by laity that gather together for word and Communion services in the absence of a priest, for discussions of the connection of the Bible to people's everyday lives, and for social activism resulting from these discussions.[3]

The concepts of empowerment and active participation are at the heart of base communities. Drawing from the writings of liberation theologians and Paulo Freire,[4] literacy courses were taught, not as a matter of teaching a specific skill, but of liberating the whole person with a new consciousness of his or her dignity as an active subject in the world, rather than a passive object that is merely acted upon. Teaching literacy in base communities is designed to give voice to the voiceless and to help people to understand their capacity to transform their social realities.

One of the nuns who had experience in base communities in a Third World country explained that she did not have a leadership role in the base community. She said,

> Priests and religious do not have leadership roles in these communities. They are made up of the people of the community. It is a lay-centered church there. It is the laity that has the power.

The nun pastors translated their experiences in the base communities of Latin America to their present parishes, which are made up of predominantly poor, blue-collar parishioners, and with a high unemployment rate. For instance, one of the nun pastors, while serving as a pastoral associate prior to her appointment, had organized a literacy program for the parishioners, many of whom had only rudimentary skills in reading and writing, both in their native language and in English. As pastor, she was constantly conveying to her parishioners her belief in their capacity as change agents. Over and over again, almost like a refrain, I heard her say to individual parishioners, "You can *do* it."

Other women pastors, married women and nuns alike, who had no Third World experience, had at least read the works of liberation theologians, and were likewise engaged in making the parishioners conscious of their gifts and encouraging them to share these gifts with the parish.[5] On a smaller scale, it seems that these women pastors are using the same principles of base communities in their parishes, even though they might not recognize it themselves. They think of themselves as serving and guiding, rather than dictating to people how they should act. Like the workers in base communities, they seek to foster relationships that are horizontal or circular, rather than vertical or hierarchical. As a result, decisions tend to be made in a democratic and participatory mode, where bishops, priests, and laity are all perceived as equal because they are all part of the people of God.

One of the nun pastors, who had not had Third World experience, used the term "faith communities." She stressed the need to enable the parishioners to be leaders in the parish faith community. In her words,

> If their leadership continued to be enabled for a number of years, I think that this parish would continue on. I see such gifts in the small community that are sometimes lost in the mob or in the big mass, and that is why I am out here, because I believe in that, and I believe I have gifts to bring out that will help them to somewhat determine their own destiny and their own self-worth as faith communities.

As mentioned earlier, the collaborative leadership style of women pastors is in contrast to the hierarchical style of previous male pastors in these parishes. These women administrators provide training in lay leadership, encourage the parishioners to become involved in the business of running the parish, and empower them to do so. Because they view the parishioners as owners of the parish and themselves as enablers, the women work very hard to include as many parishioners as possible as active participators. As one explained,

> Our styles are different. He had a different vision of his role than I have of my role as a pastor. I suppose I am more peo-ple-oriented, and by that I mean that each person has something valuable to share with everyone else and that I try to recognize that, help them identify it, and draw it out because I think that the whole parish is enriched when everyone is sharing their ability in ways of ministering to the parish. And so that we do it together, so it isn't just that one person ministers to a community, but the community is ministering to each other, and my role is to help activate that and to encourage and nurture it.

This allusion to a "different vision" runs like a theme throughout the interviews with the women pastors. This is not surprising, given the very different vantage points of priest and laity.

There are several reasons why these women are successful in their efforts to encourage the parishioners to cooperate in the running of the parish. First of all, they can identify closely with the laity, and this includes the nuns who are not members of the clergy; therefore, they, too, are nonordained pastors. There are some advantages for women who had been active parishioners before they were appointed to head the parish, as one priest explained:

> There are some things that couldn't happen with a priest there [at her parish]. For example, one thing that is very highly stressed over there is lay leadership. I can talk about that all day here [at my parish] but it doesn't have the same impact because you might have a parishioner who doesn't want to talk with Father, but will talk with [the woman pastor] because she lives down the street. When [the woman pastor] says, "Well, I'm a mother, too, and I have kids at home," or whatever, "and being the lector is something I enjoy and you would enjoy it, too," they take it in a different way than if it came from me. So in many ways she is better [than I am] with the laity because she is a laywoman. She is excellent at getting people to participate.

Another priest voiced a similar opinion about the effectiveness of religious women who had not been members of the
parish before being appointed as pastors:

> Because the sisters are doing a really good job and helping the
> people in [their parishes] to have more choice and ownership
> of what they are doing here, people see them as sort of one
> like themselves.

The ability of women pastors to restructure the parish is also
enhanced by the fact that most of their parishioners are worried
about parish survival. As I mentioned earlier, in many cases their
grandparents and great-grandparents are buried in the parish
cemetery. In a few of the parishes I visited, where the cemetery
is placed adjacent to the church, I noted graves dating back to
the mid-1800s.

In addition, some of the parishioners mentioned names of
their ancestors who had helped to build the church. They have
vivid memories of the stories told them about important contributions made by their relatives to the establishment of the
parish. Because their families have been baptized, married, and
buried in the parish, the parishioners want it to be there for the
future generation as well. The appointment of a nonpriest as
parish leader suggests to them the possibility that their parish
could close in the future, unless they become involved in keeping the parish going. Thus, they cooperated willingly in keeping
the parish open with their voluntary services.

Parishes differed in their efforts toward the development of
lay leadership, however. One parishioner complained:

> With any nonpriest-pastor situation, I think what is important
> is the development of lay leadership, lay ministry. To do that
> you cannot just grab people off the street. You have to give
> them a spirituality; you have to give them basic skills. And you
> have to either plug them into programs that are available in
> the diocese or you have to have certain ideas in mind and be
> a mentor to these people who want to be involved in lay min-
> istry. This is where our parish needs some real hard work. We
> need the structures for, not short-term development of lay min-
> istry, but long-term. We have to engage people on a short-
> term basis to help them understand they can contribute. But
> given the realities of peoples' lives, a lot of them can't make

the two-year commitment for a leadership role. But what we need to do is to get them in and get them out and build up the idea within them that they are necessary to the community.

One of the women pastors described how she has trained eight of her parishioners as presiders at the Communion services held on weekdays in their parish. They take turns presiding at these services, and the pastor herself presides only once a week. As she said, "It's *our* parish, not mine." While I visited that parish I had a chance to observe this shared leadership in action when I watched one of her parishioners presiding at a weekly Communion service. I sat in a pew with the woman pastor and watched as the parishioner greeted the people, led the prayers, read the scripture, gave a reflection on the scriptural readings, and distributed Communion. Clearly this was not a "first" for her, and the congregation seemed quite comfortable with her as presider. The pastor proudly told me after the service that this same woman had taken care of all arrangements for the funeral of a parishioner who died while she was on vacation, arranging for the Mass, contacting a priest, arranging for the liturgy, music, and readings.

In another parish the parishioners also managed funeral arrangements during the pastor's vacation:

> They [the parishioners] tried to get one priest, but they couldn't get him. The other priest was busy. The third priest said he could come for the wake but could not come for the funeral, and they said, "No, Father, we don't need you for the wake. We can do that ourselves. But we need somebody for the funeral." So, as it turned out, they did the wake themselves. And then they did get a priest for the following day for the burial.

Because of the growing shortage of priests, it becomes more important for priest-pastors to develop lay leadership in their parishes also, and there are signs that this is happening. One of the women pastors described a clergy education workshop, where she had been invited to make a presentation to the priests of the diocese. She said, "Some [priests] wanted to know what they could do to prepare their parishes, not only for alternate staffing, but also to help the laity take ownership. I thought that was a sign of life."

These women are also preparing their parishioners to take over in their absence. One of the women pastors in a very poor parish with high unemployment, who in her own way was forming base communities in her parish, described it this way:

> I feel very optimistic because I know they are already a new people. They know how to stand on their own feet. They have had experience that they are someone, that they are capable, that they can speak out. I say to them that they have to question things, to me or to the bishop. They have that right to speak out and question things. It is not any more blind faith. I know they can handle it.

These women pastors tend to be very committed to preparing the laity to take over when they are no longer there. In particular, they train the parishioners with a talent for leadership to preside at the word and Communion service, so that the parishioner-presiders can take over when they are on vacation. This "in-service training" was also extended to week-day services in some priestless parishes, as mentioned earlier. Parishioner-presiders have substituted, on occasion, for a priest who failed to show up for Mass, as this parishioner testifies:

> We have had substitute priests not show up. A priest from the home office didn't show up because he went to the wrong place. Our schedules are such that he thought he was supposed to be someplace else. We came into church and there was nobody. Everybody sat around for a few minutes and one of our parishioners who has done some presiding overseas, came forth with no notice at all and did a service, and did a really respectable job, delivered a sermon off the top of his head. And we found out if we have to we can do it.

Support Systems and Resources

Anyone seeking to enter a new role within an existing institution can expect to encounter some resistance.[1] This is especially true when the process involves a complete redefinition of role attributes and activities. Then the innovator is by definition questioning certain widely held assumptions about the role. While women pastors experience constraints and tensions, there are resources available to them as they meet the obstacles to the successful performance of their new role. In particular, support systems exist in the form of aid and encouragement offered by bishops, priests, and parishioners, as well as other resources both inside and outside the diocese.

BISHOPS

Data regarding the support of the local bishop are based on the interviewees' perceptions of his support. Although I did not interview the local bishops, I asked how the woman pastor, the sacramental minister, and the parishioners assessed the bishop's support.[2] Thus all the interviewees were asked if they thought the bishop was supportive of the woman pastor's presence in the parish. Also, the women pastors, priests, and parishioners were asked to describe how the bishop showed support or non-support for her activities.

Some of the interviewees said that their bishop evidenced support at the earliest phase of the recruitment process, at the point when a parish was first designated for alternate staffing.

This designation meant that the parish would soon have a deacon or a nonordained person as its resident pastor. The initial support took different forms, but it usually involved the bishop himself making a visit to the parish, where he consulted with the parishioners before completing the recruitment process. As might be expected, the bishop's effort to involve the parishioners in this initial phase of the process paved the way for the arrival of the woman pastor.

The most dramatic example of this early support was related by a male parishioner. In his account, corroborated by others, he stated that the bishop asked the retiring pastor to announce to the parishioners that he would arrive on a specified day to meet with them to explain his plans for the parish. This event was described as a public forum open to all. Parishioners were encouraged to bring questions to the meeting.

The parishioner who described the bishop's visit attended the meeting, and he estimated that thirty parishioners (in a parish of 145 families) were there ("a good turnout"). During the meeting the bishop made it clear to the parishioners that it was *his* decision to appoint a layperson as head of the parish. He explained his reasons for this decision, and opened the meeting for questions from the floor. After answering questions posed by the parishioners, the bishop said, "Now, here's my telephone number." After repeating his number, he then reminded the parishioners that it was *his* decision to designate the parish for alternate staffing. He then instructed the parishioners to phone or come to him directly if they had problems with his decision, and not to whomever was appointed to head the parish.

The time and effort to travel to the parish and the long meeting with the parishioners were evidence of the bishop's support, but the fact that he took personal responsibility for the decision to designate the parish for alternate staffing added to the strength of his support of the lay pastor. Although the quality and quantity of initial support on the part of this particular bishop was a unique occurrence in the parishes I visited, the consequences were so dramatic for the lay pastor that the event merits emphasis.

In addition to meeting with the bishop, some of the parishioners in the same parish were involved in a later phase of the recruitment process, when they interviewed prospective candidates for the position. Because they had a chance to meet the candidates and the parishioners' input was solicited, one parishioner said, "They were very favorable" when the final choice was made. However, on reflecting on the recruitment process, my informant told me that he was convinced that by taking a "strong, no-nonsense position" at a very early stage in the process, the bishop made the adjustment to the new role much easier for the lay pastor.

Some bishops also sought the advice of the parish council in the prerecruiting phase. One priest said,

> [The bishop] has tried and is increasingly allowing for the advice of the parish councils. Through official letters to them with a questionnaire, he will get back from them what the needs of the parish are, and what they are looking for in terms of a pastoral leader. I know for a fact it has had [a] great impact on him about what kind of person should be selected.

One of the women pastors explained that the bishop sent a representative from the diocesan personnel office who met with the parishioners and "tried to develop a process to help them to deal with the fact that they weren't going to have a priest, and what did that mean." In another parish, a parishioner told me that the bishop came into a parish council meeting soon after the appointment of the woman pastor. On that occasion the bishop answered questions from council members, and then at the end of the meeting he legitimated her position in the parish by saying, "I have assigned her here, and she is here."

An additional resource for the lay pastor can be provided by the bishop after the candidate has been chosen, and the appointment had been made. This support, often initiated by the bishop, but sometimes by the parishioners or by the pastor herself with the bishop's approval, takes the form of an installation ceremony. The ceremony usually occurred during the first two or three months following the new pastor's arrival. It took place as a public ritual in the parish church with the bishop or his representative presiding. The principal function of the installation ceremony is the legitimation of the new pastor's leadership. I asked every interviewee if there had been an installation ceremony, and if so, to describe it.

About half of the pastors had been formally "installed" by the bishop. After speaking about the installation ceremony with pastors and parishioners, it became clear that the women pastors viewed it as a form of very positive support because they saw it as a conferring of public ecclesiastical approval on them in their new role.

The most dramatic example of the support afforded by an installation ceremony occurred in a parish where the nun pastor had previously served for four years as a pastoral associate in charge of religious education. In this case the bishop informed the new pastor when the installation was to take place, and asked her to involve the parishioners in designing the ceremony itself.

The parishioners not only chose the appropriate readings and hymns, but also wrote into the ceremony the symbolic moment when the power was to be passed on to the pastor. According to the program for the ceremony that was printed and distributed to the congregation, a parishioner was to give the processional cross to the bishop, who turned to the woman pastor and said, "I present you with the visible sign that unites this people. Take this cross as a symbol of the ministries of this community. It is the burden and glory of those who seek to love and serve Christ." Her response was, "On behalf of all who minister here at [the parish], I accept this cross as a sign of God's eternal and embracing love." The printed instructions stated that she was then to raise the cross before the people. As she was recounting that experience, tears welled up into her eyes. In her words,

> It was a very joyful affair, and the part that I think stands out the most for me was that after the homily [by the bishop] at the official installation time in the ceremony, one of the ushers was supposed to bring up the processional cross, and I was to simply raise it. Just as that happened, Bishop _____ whispered to me, "Sister, you can bless the whole community if you want to." So instead of simply raising it—I hardly knew what I was doing, to tell you the truth because I wasn't quite expecting that—I made the sign of the cross, and it was a very moving time. I could see lots of people with tears. It was a very joyful time. At that point it was very spontaneous, the applause afterwards. The whole community was caught up in it, and it was beautiful. I think it was a standing ovation. There was a lot of clapping.

When I asked her how the bishop responded to her blessing, she said that she was so shocked by the bishop's invitation
that she couldn't remember how she did it, but somehow she
managed not only to raise the cross, but to bless the congregation as well. She was able to describe the parishioners' response,
but she was so nervous about her first public blessing that she
did not observe what the bishop's response was. Luckily the ceremony had been videotaped, and I had time to view the tape
before I concluded my visit at her parish. The videotape showed
that the bishop himself received her blessing; that is, he made
the sign of the cross (blessed himself) as she blessed the congregation with the processional cross. This was a dramatic recognition of her legitimate authority on his part; in fact it could be
described very aptly as a ritual that "worked."

When I described to the woman pastor what I had seen on
the tape, her first reaction was shock and disbelief. However,
after she sorted it out, she rejoiced at his unexpected response.
She then interpreted the bishop's reception of her blessing as a
partial explanation of the parishioners' standing ovation.

Equally important, symbolically, was the fact that the processional cross, which had been carried in by a member of the
parish council, was passed from a parishioner to the bishop,
who in turn gave it to her. This procedure was written into the
ceremony by the parishioners, and it represented a direct
involvement of the parishioners in the conferring of that authority on her. In fact, it suggested that the conferring of authority
began with the parishioners, and passed then to the bishop,
who finally conferred it upon her.

Most of the other installation ceremonies were described as
more modest affairs. For instance, a woman pastor said,

> It was a very simple ceremony, the vicar general and sacra-
> mental minister and myself. We processed in. It was just a very
> simple ceremony. After the homily I was called up and
> received a candle as a symbol of leading the people, and then
> was asked some questions.

Another form of support can be found in the contracts
between the bishop and the women pastors. The terms of the
contract varied from diocese to diocese, but the supportive bish-

ops tended to specify three or six years as the appointment period, with the possibility of renewing the contract for an additional three or six years. In many cases the women were given the same appointment period as the former priest-pastors.

Once the women were appointed and installed as the leaders of the parish, most of the bishops continued to support them in a variety of ways. Sometimes it was in the form of a public statement. One bishop, according to a lay pastor, "keeps telling people that this [appointing laity to head parishes] is the way of the future." Many parishioners reported that the bishop often thanked the woman pastor publicly for her work in the parish. In particular at the ceremony of confirmation in the parish, many parishioners and priests stated that the bishop thanked her for her work in the parish, and complimented her on the way she prepared the children for the sacrament.

A parishioner described her bishop's support thus:

> When he was here I know he did make the remarks about Sister _____ as far as the role in the parish and how good she was doing. I don't remember exactly what he said, but I know we had a service with the bishop for the anointing of the sick, and he came for that. I know he did make remarks then about things Sister _____ was doing in the parish. I know he is really happy with what she is doing.

Another parishioner described a "town meeting" with the bishop:

> The last time he [the bishop] was here we had a potluck meal. Everybody showed up and we had a town meeting and people asked questions. He said, "You know, you have a terrific person leading you, and I can see by this turnout how well she is supported." So he verbally on occasions has come here and said, "You have a terrific person, I am proud of her, she is doing an outstanding job."

One of the women pastors said that the bishop always affirmed her in public. On one occasion when he came to the parish while she was away on vacation, the parishioners told her that the bishop really supported her. In her words,

> They [the parishioners] said something about the Catholic Church doesn't have women priests. And he [the bishop] said,

"You're right, and [she] is not a woman priest, but she might as well be."

One parishioner said that the bishop both privately and publicly "went out of his way to use the word 'Pastor.' He says, '[she] is your pastor.'" Another woman said that she was listed as pastor in the Diocesan Catholic Directory, something that would not have happened without the approval of the bishop.

One lay pastor showed me the tape of the bishop's formal dedication of her new church building and grounds. In the procession to and from the blessing of the cemetery she and the priest walked side by side directly in front of the bishop. Later, when the bishop was given the key to the church, he said, "I'd better give it to the pastor." And the bishop handed the key to the woman pastor, who unlocked the door.

This incident and the two mentioned in the paragraphs above may seem inconsequential, but such manifestations on the part of the bishop can be extremely important in establishing the woman pastor's legitimacy with her parishioners.

Some bishops also showed their support in a less public way. As a woman pastor explained,

> The other way he has shown support is about once a year he gives me a telephone call and he'll just kind of ask how things are going in the parish and how I'm doing. And that's been nice. He doesn't grill me with questions but just generally wants to know how things are going in the parish and what new things are going on. More of a concern than a questioning.

In the event that the sacramental minister cannot be present for the Sunday Mass and is unable to find a substitute priest, some bishops authorize the woman pastor to lead a service of God's Word and Holy Communion, often referred to as a "word and communion service." While this service is not, strictly speaking, a Mass, the bishop often helps the woman pastor by making it clear to the parishioners that the word and communion service led by their lay pastor serves as the parish community's Sunday celebration and fulfills their Sunday Mass obligation. In fact, one of the bishops instructed the woman pastor to post the following letter in the vestibule [foyer] of the church and missions which she was administering:

When the priests at _____ are unable to celebrate Sunday
Masses at _____ and its missions, either because of illness or
bad weather, and no other priest is available, Sister should
conduct the Liturgy of the Word with a reflection talk[3] and
appropriate prayers for the distribution of Holy Communion.
In these instances, this Sunday service will enable the people
to fulfill their Sunday obligation of worship.

Another way a bishop can support his woman pastor is by
treating her as if she is the one in charge when he visits the
parish. Many of the parishioners mentioned this type of affirming behavior on the part of their bishop.

Another support, and a very practical one at that, is the bishop's willingness to substitute for the priest [sacramental minister]
when he is sick or on vacation. One of the women pastors said
that her bishop came to her parish to say Mass five or six times
a year; another said that her bishop came to the parish whenever she invited him, and would even give her feedback on her
homilies when she sent them to him.

One of the priests spoke of the support given to women in
general by his bishop. He described it this way:

When Bishop _____ gave his guidelines out for eucharistic
ministers, he said that every woman has to wear an alb[4] if they
want to be a eucharistic minister. I don't know his reasoning
behind it, but I thought to myself, he is reaffirming the role of
women in a liturgical setting.

Another priest described his bishop's stance as feminist
when he explained that the bishop seeks out parishes where he
can place a woman. He said that this is a deliberate move on the
part of the bishop, because he wants more women as pastors. In
at least two of the dioceses I visited, I discovered that there was
a diocesan policy of not ordaining deacons, because to do so
would rule out leadership roles for women.[5]

One of the women pastors who often had difficulty finding
priests to administer the sacraments in her parish told about
admitting to the bishop that she had, on occasion, administered
the sacrament of baptism herself. She quoted her bishop's
affirming response thus: "You've got to do what you've got to
do, and if that's what needs to be done at the time, that's your
pastoral duty."

These instances that indicate support on the part of bishops were described to me very enthusiastically by lay pastors, priests, and parishioners. They all seemed to sense that these words and actions of the bishop represented an important source of legitimation for the new pastors. However, some bishops are more supportive than others; in fact, the level of support varies from very supportive to supportive to neutral to nonsupportive. As I mentioned earlier, the bishops divide equally on this dimension, with half [seven] on the supportive side and the other half [seven] on the neutral or nonsupportive side. The next chapter will elaborate on the neutral and nonsupportive bishops. Now we turn to the supports provided by priests, and in particular, by the sacramental minister assigned to the parish.

PRIESTS

The relationship between the woman pastor and the priest who provides sacramental ministry is an extremely sensitive one, and it is fraught with potential tensions, constraints, and conflicts. Because of parishioners' high regard for the priest, he has the power, wittingly or unwittingly, to undermine the authority of the woman pastor in the parish. On the other hand, because of the parishioners' veneration of his priesthood, the sacramental minister also has the potential to support her position when he visits the parish by his words and actions.

When I interviewed the sacramental ministers, I asked each one how he supported her leadership in the parish. I also asked each of the women pastors how, in her view, the sacramental minister supported her parish leadership, and I asked the same question of the parishioners. Because I not only interviewed the sacramental ministers, but in many cases was able to observe them in action on the weekend, I thus have an additional source of data regarding the priest's support.

How did these priests lend support to the leadership of the women pastors? Many of them see to it that the woman pastor is physically placed in a position of equality during the church services, and I saw this in action at many of the parishes I visited. As one of the priests described it,

We walk up [to the altar] together in the opening procession.
We preside together. In fact, lately I open the Mass with the
sign of the cross, and she will do the penitential rite, and then
the opening prayer. And then above and beyond that, of
course, if she is preaching that weekend it would be the homily. I think she has a nice presence for the sake of the people,
and she is the pastor here, for all intents and purposes.

When observing during Mass at these parishes, I often
watched the priest and woman pastor walk in procession up the
aisle side by side, and take their places in the sanctuary next to
each other. Her voice was often the first heard by the congregation, because the service began when she greeted the congregation and gave a short commentary on the theme of the day's
liturgy. The woman pastor often read the scriptures and/or
preached the sermon, and sometimes she distributed Communion alongside the priest. Her voice would often be the last
heard, when she made the announcements at the end of Mass.
The supportive priests showed by their demeanor that they not
only approved of her near-equal status, but that they recognized
and affirmed her leadership role in the parish.

Another priest described their sharing of the baptismal rite:

At baptisms she has a prominent role to play in the rites. She
will do the questioning of parents and godparents, all of those
initial prayers, the blessing of the water. She will be present
for the actual baptism of the child and the signing of the
chrism.[6]

A woman pastor described her participation in a baptism:

Father _____ did let me participate in the baptism. I introduced them, called them by name, asked some of the questions.

In one parish the priest had a very egalitarian relationship
with the pastor, but she was reluctant to preach during Mass.
The priest explained how he interpreted the bishop's homily at
her installation ceremony, and thus his rationale for urging her
to preach.

In his [the bishop's] homily, he was really commissioning her
to be leader of the parish, spiritually and in every other way,
and to teach. As I heard it that day I said to myself, "Aha, if

she's going to teach, she's going to have to preach, because if he's commissioning this woman to teach, that means she'll have to preach." Most of your folks are there on Sunday, and if you're not talking to them you're not communicating anything to your parish. So I thought, "Aha, good."

Like some of the bishops mentioned in the section above, there were also priests who referred to the woman as "pastor." In the words of a woman pastor, "Sometimes priests will call me and tell me I am the pastor. Lots of them do that." One of the sacramental ministers said, "When people ask me what her position is, I tell them she is the pastor of the church."

In some of the parishes, the parishioners would wait until the priest arrived on the weekend, and then bombard him with the kinds of questions and requests that should have more appropriately been addressed to the woman pastor. The priest's response to these questions and requests is critical, because it can help to make or break the acceptance of the woman's position in the parish. A supportive strategy used by many of the priests was to make it clear that she was, indeed, the pastor of the parish. One of the priests said:

> In regard to acceptance, when we [he and the woman pastor] were first here the first months, they [the parishioners] would often still stop and ask me questions instead of her. I would plead ignorance and I said, "That's not my role. Sister is it, so it would be most important to talk to her." So, certainly within the last eighteen months no one really asks me questions. I don't go to parish council meetings or anything like that.

A woman pastor explained the same strategy used by her sacramental ministers:

> If the parishioners go to them with something they should be going to me about, they [the priests] immediately refer them to me.... They [a family in the parish] tried to catch him [the priest] and ask him if they could have a baptism outside the Mass, and he said, "Go ask your pastor. If she says yes, I will do it."

One of the woman pastors said that the priests who served as sacramental ministers for her parish were very supportive. She said, "They [the priests] make it clear to the people by their comments that I am in charge. The priests will refer to me as 'your pastor.'"

This same priest's stance on the altar underlined his support of her position. While the woman pastor was preaching one Sunday, he focused his whole attention on her words, turning and facing her throughout the sermon. He was a good role model for the parishioners, for his body language proclaimed to the congregation that they should pay attention to their pastor's message to them.

One of the parishioners explained this same priest's strategy this way:

> Father was very quick to support everything that Sister was doing, and he tried to offer an explanation as to why. But when it came right down to it, it was, "Do it, folks, because she's not doing it because she wants to; she's doing it in your best interest." And he was very supportive of her.

In addition to the priests who are the sacramental ministers for the parish, the support of a previous pastor who was highly esteemed by the parishioners can also be an important resource for the woman pastor. One of the married women who had been a parishioner before her assignment as pastor, told me that the previous pastor encouraged her to attend classes on all aspects of pastoral ministry a few years before her appointment. In a few of the parishes I visited, the previous priest-pastors had met with the parish council to prepare them for the arrival of the woman pastor, and others used their homilies at Mass prior to the arrival of the woman pastor for the same purpose.

In one case the previous pastor helped to design the liturgy for her installation ceremony, and took an active part in it. As the woman pastor described it,

> He [the previous pastor] handed me the scripture, telling me I would be the spiritual leader of the community. He handed me a rosary which was a very prominent devotion here for the people. Those were the symbols. Also, he handed me the checkbook, saying I would have the responsibility of keeping the place going, and the bills paid. The last thing [the priest] handed over to me were the people.

Another priest who had previously been pastor at the parish, assessed the success of the current woman pastor in this way.

I ran that place for seven years. But I really think it is running better today. The church is full. Things are better than they ever were when I was pastor. That place has grown in wisdom, age, and grace. And the people are really participating. I didn't have that when I was pastor.

PARISHIONERS

While the bishop's and priest's support are important resources, they alone could not offer adequate support to a new pastor. After all, the parishioners interact with the pastor on a daily basis, and without their help and/or encouragement she would be ineffective.

Parishioner support of women pastors takes a variety of forms. One would assume that initial manifestations of parishioners' help and encouragement would spring from deeply held convictions and feelings about their responsibility to support their local pastor. We would also expect such support to be forthcoming from those who had strongly held convictions about gender equality. Later on, as parishioners learn to love and respect her as a person, we would also expect their help to be forthcoming. However, parishioners' support is also offered for a pragmatic reason—the fear that their church might close. In this section we will examine both parishioners's feelings and actions that serve as a support to the woman pastor.

A female parishioner described her feelings about the appointment of her woman pastor:

> I felt at that point when Father _____ was here, he had two parishes and it was a lot of work for him. And I know when he talked about Sister coming and helping out as our pastoral administrator I felt good about it because he really had an overload. I felt it was important that the women should play a role, have some role in the Church. I felt really good about it. I felt good that she was coming here.

Another parishioner said,

> I think this is the best thing that ever has happened here. I like to say when [she] moved in, the spirit moved in with her. We have seen more growth; we have seen people grow closer together; we have just that spirit that never was here before.

People are beginning to participate more, to volunteer more readily, to be friendlier. And I am speaking as an outsider. It is a closed community, I feel, and we've been here for twenty-five years, and I always felt [as an] outsider. And now we are beginning to feel like we belong here, and this all came about after [she] was here.

Parishioners sometimes showed their support even before her arrival at the parish by cleaning and renovating the parish house. In one such parish a female parishioner said,

> There were some repairs that had to be done on the house when [she] came, and there were people who helped with it. A lot of people came and helped before she came, to clean the house and get everything cleaned up and ready for her to live there.

One woman pastor mentioned that her parishioners welcomed her to the parish by organizing potluck dinners two or three weeks after she arrived. She saw it as their way of getting better acquainted with her.

Soon after the arrival of the woman pastor, parishioners tended to offer their help as they assessed her needs. For instance, in a parish where the pastor was a young married woman with small children, a parishioner told me that people were "volunteering like crazy to help with the kids." The pastor herself told me that she never had to worry about child care.

A male parishioner described a variety of supportive actions on the part of parishioners:

> We have a small parish here, and of course, financially we are not able to have a custodian. We have cleaning teams made up of people that alternate taking care of the church. We have ladies that come in and make the flower arrangements for the altar. Just about anything that needs to be done has to be done on a volunteer basis. We had people come and trim the shrubs recently. I had volunteer work to build that ramp [an access to the church for the handicapped]. That was all built since Sister _____ was here with volunteer labor. A lot of times they will have cleaning bees for special occasions like Christmas or Easter, and the ladies will turn out for that. Sometimes there will be a small cleaning bee in the church cemetery.

One of the male parishioners told me that even the non-Catholic husband of a parishioner often shoveled the walk to the parish house. He added,

> There's always somebody around [to help]. Sometimes I'll come around and take the blower out. Three or four ladies count the collection on Monday morning.

Contributions of food were a regular occurrence in rural parishes. One of the women pastors told me that the parishioners brought her a lot of produce from their gardens, and the very next day, while we were sitting in the kitchen drinking coffee, a parishioner stopped by with several bags of fresh vegetables. She said that she never refuses any of this food so as not to hurt the parishioner's feelings. Instead she either gives it away, cans it, or freezes what she cannot immediately use.

Another woman pastor stated:

> They continued to be so generous with their garden foods. I don't think I was here three days when I got a big bag of corn. It just made me feel like they would want me to stay.

Another lay pastor, in describing how food often appeared almost miraculously, said, "We find food on the porch—a peach pie, tomatoes. One time we found it in the back of the car."

One of the parishioners mentioned that his pastor received many gifts from various parishioners at Christmastime. In another parish a woman pastor who had unexpected surgery told me how thrilled she was at the outpouring of flowers, etc., from the parishioners. She said that she received over one hundred get well cards from the parishioners, and so many flowers that she was afraid she wouldn't have enough space in her hospital room. Another pastor said that she also viewed her parishioners' expressions of gratitude as a form of gift to her.

Another support comes in the form of invitations to share a meal with a family in the parish, especially on the occasion of a birthday, an anniversary, or other family celebrations. One of the married lay pastors, who was beginning to feel overwhelmed by the numbers of such invitations, said,

> Sometimes it's really hard. We had three Saturdays in a row where we had to go out after Mass for these family celebra-

tions. As time goes cn, you can see it happening more and more. It's great; you really feel loved, but...

A sister who lived alone in the parish house had this to say about the invitations:

> And there is support in [the parishioners] just being friendly and inviting me out to different occasions. They want me to be part of their family gatherings. The fourth of July, for instance, a whole family reunion was happening. Memorial Day, Christmas. Many people check [me] out, "Are you going to be home?" They don't want me to be here by myself and would like me to be part of their family gathering. [They] really want me to be part of the parish family. I feel real well accepted and liked.

Some of the dioceses have guidelines for lay pastors which specify that they should wear an alb on any occasion when they are expected to take their place in the sanctuary, with or without a priest. This presents a dilemma for women, because albs for Catholic priests are made for men. In two of the parishes I visited the parishioners made the alb themselves and presented it to their pastor. In another parish the members of the Women's Guild, with the help of the local Methodist minister, purchased a female alb for their pastor from a Methodist catalogue. As the pastor herself described it, "The Women's Guild, without even asking me, offered to buy me an alb, because I was wearing all those men's things that looked just terrible on me."

Two very important indicators of parishioner support—the bottom line, as it were—are attendance at Mass and weekly financial contributions. Most of the parishioners whom I interviewed stated that their parish experienced an increase in numbers at Mass and in contributions to the Sunday collection soon after their pastor arrived. Several also mentioned that fund-raising events had been successful since her arrival. In most parishes the amount of the previous Sunday's collection are published in the church bulletin, so that the parishioners are able to chart the increased giving. They could also see the evidence regarding church attendance and participation in religious education classes in the enrollment figures and in the numbers of people kneeling in the pews on Sundays.

For instance, a female parishioner in a parish where the previous pastor had been semiretired and where a young woman pastor and her husband had recently been appointed as copastors described it this way:

> We had about eighty-four or eighty-five families before [they] came, and now I think our enrollment is 111 families. It shot right up. There are a lot of kids and a lot of very young families, and more since [they] came. Our CCD[7] enrollment, our Christian youth classes have really increased. There are definitely more people at Mass now, more people at everything, and more people doing things.

A male parishioner in another parish said,

> I would think there is a little bit more [money] given since Sister came and everything stabilized. She never asks for anything personally. Within the next few months we started a building fund. We knew where the monies were going, and they weren't being wasted.... She didn't have a microwave and we gave her one. She didn't ask for one. She didn't ask for anything.

One of the women pastors attested to her parishioners' support in this way:

> They give a good [amount of] time commitment. The contributions have risen a lot. Attendance has increased dramatically. And people are affirming.... I feel a satisfaction in seeing attendance go up and seeing the income go up.

A female parishioner summed up the support in her parish in this way:

> I personally see it as an affirmation when I see people stepping forward and doing things [in the parish]. A lot of people who have been there in the pews for twenty years [seemed] like bumps on a log, and now they are beginning to do things. I think that's affirming. More and more, after Mass people want to stop and talk to her. There will be a group of people waiting to see her after Mass. I think that's good and affirming because it used to be they were all gone immediately.

The final form of parishioner support that I will mention is a verbal one, which I heard at virtually every parish I visited. It is simply this: THEY CALL HER PASTOR. Here are some examples:

A female parishioner, in describing her to me, simply stated, "She is our pastor." A·nun pastor said,

> When they [the parishioners] introduce me to people, they always say, "This is our pastor." And they do refer to me as their pastor, and I know this because I have heard it from other people.

A married pastor explained,

> Usually they'll say, "Oh, she's our pastor," or "She's our minister." It's usually in those terms. Some of them have gotten into the hang of saying pastoral administrator, but they usually will just say, "She's our lay pastor, or our pastor."

Each time I heard a woman explain how her parishioners usually referred to her as their pastor, I noted that it was said with much pride and with a smile. They all know that the title "pastor" is reserved solely for priests, but their experience in the parish has convinced them that in spite of that institutional constraint they are, indeed, pastors in the true sense of the word. And like true pastors, their reason for accepting the job and for remaining in the position, in spite of the constraints, conflicts, and tensions, resides in their parishioners. To my question, "What is it that keeps you going in your ministry?" the answer, unanimous and unequivocal, was "The parishioners." Here are two examples of their responses. The first is from a sister who said,

> I ask myself that a lot of times. I really am very energized. A lot of times it is on a person-to-person level. When I see new life happening, and that I could be part of that happening, or new levels of faith happening in them, excitement about themselves, excitement about their parish, more belief in themselves, more self-identity, a better image of themselves and also as a parish—this is a real plus for me. I guess I have always compared it to giving birth. That gives birth to me, when that happens. And open-mindedness: a futuristic look, open to new aspects, especially when I see new leadership happen among them, and they start to identify, and to own.

A married lay pastor put it this way:

If it wasn't for the people, I don't think I would stay, because I would say somebody else can go be on the cutting edge for awhile, and take care of the headaches and hassles. I think what would keep me from leaving this parish is some of the relationships we've already developed with the people. And I feel like I can't leave these people like that, despite any other difficulties that might come along.

OTHER RESOURCES

In addition to the supports provided by their bishops, priests, and parishioners, two types of networks also serve as resources for the women pastors. The first can be found in the Office of Ministry which has been established in many of the dioceses throughout the country. Often this office not only provides in-service training, but staff from the diocesan office will answer questions by telephone as they arise, and will sometimes visit the parish when called on by the woman pastor. The director of this office or, in some cases, the personnel director, will also schedule periodic group meetings of lay pastors, and this group can become an important resource. One woman pastor described such a meeting:

> The other thing we do is meet monthly with the pastoral administrators, and our agenda is, "What are some of the things we are having questions and problems with?" And then we get either the vicar general[8] to come in and talk about some of these things, or address a certain topic, or get somebody from the state to talk about some legal issues. So we do get some of those questions answered through some of the meetings and speakers that we have, or people that come in and share.

As the women reported, the more important function of such meetings was the opportunity to meet and know their counterparts from other parishes in the diocese. As a result of these meetings, several of them communicate regularly by telephone. About five of the women interviewed were the only lay pastors in their dioceses, and all of them expressed their disappointment that such a resource was unavailable to them.

The second resource mentioned by many of the women I interviewed is the Institute for Pastoral Life, based in Kansas

City, Missouri, which I briefly described in chapter 1.[9] This center, established by some Catholic bishops in 1985, offers a three-year training program for parish life coordinators [their term for lay pastors] from poor rural parishes. It lasts for two weeks, and is held during the summer in Kansas City.[10] In addition to the summer training program, the Institute for Pastoral Life also publishes a newsletter that often includes articles written by lay pastors throughout the country. It also occasionally sponsors teleconferences and symposia on various aspect of lay ministry, and makes available videotapes of these meetings.

Twelve of the women I interviewed had attended the two-week institute in Kansas City for three summers, and they were very enthusiastic about their participation in this program, primarily because it gave them the opportunity to share their experiences with other women pastors throughout the country. As some of them expressed it to me, if this program provided nothing more than the acquaintance of other women pastors, it was well worth their time and effort. After spending two full weeks for three summers together, some of them developed important friendships with other women pastors throughout the country, and they continue to communicate with each other by letter or by telephone.

This chapter has shown that in some instances bishops, priests, and parishioners can provide some support for women pastors, and that several of them have also benefited from diocesan and national support networks. However, we have been looking with rose-colored glasses at the woman pastor's relationships. In order to see the entire picture we need to look beyond the supports and resources, and examine the other side of the coin, the constraints, conflicts, and tensions experienced by women in this position.

•7•

Constraints, Conflicts, and Tensions

No matter how supportive the bishop, priest, and parishioners may be, no matter how many other resources she may have, there are built-in constraints for the woman pastor that persist in spite of all of the supports available to her.[1] These institutional constraints, in turn, often lead to conflicts and tensions in her everyday life. The role of lay pastor of a priestless parish is not only a new role, but it is one that has been redefined to exclude some of the key duties of previous pastors. Assuming that parishioners and priests share the desire to keep the parish operating, we would expect cooperation, rather than conflict, to predominate. However, conflict and tension can arise from a lack of any definition regarding what constitutes "appropriate behavior" for the woman pastor. In particular, the circumstances surrounding the liturgical and sacramental functions are especially sensitive.

In fact, the role of woman pastor is fraught with ambiguity that can be a constant source of strain in her daily relationships with parishioners and priests. In order to understand the role ambiguities involved in the relationships between women pastors and their role partners, it is necessary to shed some light on the institutional constraints placed on the activities of the women in this new leadership position.

The primary source of these conflicts and tensions is, of course, on the institutional level. It is the combination of teachings, laws, policies, and practices of the Catholic church that prohibit the woman appointed to head a parish from exercising all the powers of a priest-pastor. In earlier chapters I have alluded to some of these institutional constraints in the lives of the women I interviewed, but I will elaborate on the nature of these constraints in the first section of this chapter. The rest of the chapter will examine the consequences of these constraints in the daily encounters of women pastors with priests, bishops, and their parishioners; and how these women, their parishioners, and sacramental ministers think and feel about these constraints.

INSTITUTIONAL CONSTRAINTS:
CHURCH TEACHINGS, LAWS, AND PRACTICES

The chief institutional constraint for the woman pastor results from a law of the church which restricts priestly ordination to males, so that even though they are doing the work of a priest-pastor in these parishes, they are not, and cannot be members of the clergy. In the final analysis, then, a woman pastor is not a priest, and her nonordained status is the bottom line that places her in a position which, in institutional church terms, carries a liability from the outset. Her position is "in the red," as it were. Continuing the financial analogy, we can say that her liabilities may be perceived as exceeding her assets, because she does not and cannot have the "proper" credentials.

If women could be ordained deacons, which present church law does not allow, then they would have the right to give homilies, to baptize, and to preside at marriages outside of Mass.[2] In one of the parishes I visited I found that this constraint was particularly painful for a woman pastor whose husband, with whom she was copastoring, was to be ordained a deacon in a few months. She was well aware that, as an ordained deacon, he would then have a higher status in the parish, and this would mark an end to their equal sharing of the position.

Because women pastors, including nuns, are officially laypersons, some of the central pastoral duties, such as the celebration of Mass, hearing confessions, baptizing, and presiding at marriages and funeral Masses are reserved for the sacramental minister, the "real" priest. On these occasions, when the woman must take a "back seat," the limitations in her new role are quite evident to her and to the parishioners.

A major bone of contention in many of the parishes I visited, is the role of the woman pastor in the Sunday liturgy. The built-in constraint results from the way her role has been circumscribed by the church. As one priest explained it:

> Obviously it's an auxiliary role simply because of the way the Catholic setup is. We've tried to create a style so that she has some appropriate prominent [role]. She greets the people, I don't. The first words that go through the mike to the folks are from her. She welcomes them and welcomes visitors, and talks about the theme for the day. Then I walk to the microphone and say the prayer of the day, and then the liturgy goes on.

These limitations follow her, even when a woman pastor travels outside her parish. One of the pastors reported the following incident. A priest who taught at the diocesan seminary invited her to give a talk there, but attempted to circumvent the issue of her preaching. As she explained it to me,

> He didn't say, "Preach." He said, "Talk about what you are doing." And I said, "When am I doing this, at the lunch?" And he said, "No, at Mass." I said, "What time in the Mass?" And he said, "Well, at the homily time." I said, "You say I'm preaching, then." "Well, no," he said, "I can't." I said, "I can't speak after the gospel without preaching, whether you want to call it preaching or addressing. I can't just get up and talk about something that is divorced from the gospel, because I have enough of a liturgical background to know that I don't believe that ought to be done." So he said, okay, he would stand up and say something. So he did. And then nobody could stand up and say Sister _____ preached at [the seminary]. Father _____ said three or four sentences first.

What "game," you might ask, was the priest in the above incident playing? Strictly speaking, laypersons are not permitted to preach at Mass immediately after the gospel has been read, which is "homily time." In order to avoid this prohibition, the presiding priest sometimes says a few words immediately after the gospel, and then invites a layperson to preach. The priest in the example above was circumventing the prohibition.

According to church law, the right to preach during Mass is conferred at the time a man is ordained a deacon, so it is an exclusive privilege of ordained deacons and priests. As we have seen, however, this law is open to interpretation, as is evident from the following argument from a sacramental minister:

> We can't have church without priests because then we aren't sacramental, and the Catholic church is a sacramental church. We would just simply be congregational without the priests. Obviously I am biased, but I think priests have a very important role in the church, and [the woman pastor] does not want to take my job away from me. She is quite happy to let me do my part and that is why we don't have a competition or a clash because she is happy to let me do my sacramental role, I am quite happy to let her fulfill her role and I don't see a problem with that. In fact, my allowing her to preach once a month, I think, says very clearly that [it] is not something I see as a threat to my priesthood.

A sacramental minister in another parish, however, felt differently about the situation. His more traditional stance dictated that he should ask permission before allowing the woman pastor to "cross the line," as it were. He said,

> My impression in all the years I have been involved in the church and parish work has been that when people see people doing things, then the question doesn't become, "Should we or shouldn't we?" It is more or less, "They are doing all this stuff, why can't they be ordained?" And a lot of women I have worked with have elicited that response from people. To me that is really important because I think there is a lot of anger tied up for a lot of women with the institutional church which gets transferred to priests, and then we sort of take it in the shorts for being part of the institution because we are priests. And yet there [are] a lot of limitations on us. As much as I would love to ask for permission for sisters to do things like baptisms or witness weddings and so forth, we don't have that permission here yet.

Phrases like "allowing her to preach" and "asking permission for" underline the institutional constraints placed on the role of woman pastor. In addition to the limitations placed on them in their liturgical and sacramental roles, two additional constraints concern title and dress.

About half of the women I visited have the title "pastoral administrators," some are called "pastoral coordinators," a few are "parish ministers," and one each has the title of "pastoral director," "parish lay administrator," and "parish life coordinator." Why is there such a variety in titles for these women who are pastoring parishes? Although they bear the responsibility of pastoring a parish community in their exercise of overall responsibility for worship, education, pastoral services, and administration of the parish, the title of pastor is restricted, by church law, to ordained priests, and at the present time no nationwide title has officially been bestowed on them; thus the title differs from diocese to diocese.

One could argue that there are very few examples of a role that has been so thoroughly monopolized by men as that of a Roman Catholic priest, who is typically called "Father," a title that explicitly excludes women. As we saw in the preceding chapter, however, parishioners, priests, and even bishops sometimes refer to these women as "pastor," and many of them receive mail from the diocesan office addressed to "pastor" or "reverend."

The significance of "naming" of their parishioners by women pastors as an important and positive attribute was discussed in chapter 3. Similarly, "naming" by title is significant for those so named with regard to role definition. Thus, the role ambiguity experienced by these women is both reflected and partly determined by the confusion in "naming" them.

The various titles for lay pastors were bothersome to many of the people I interviewed. For instance, one lay pastor, expressing dissatisfaction with the title, said,

> This is the typical institutional church [saying], "We can't call these people 'pastor'." Well, what are we? If a banana's a banana, you call it a banana. Why do they have to come up with pastoral administrator, parish director, pastoral agent? What are we doing? We're doing the ministry of pastor, right? Then call us that and simplify it.

In regard to the question of dress, the clerical collar can be worn by women clergy in Protestant denominations, but it cannot be worn by the women pastors in this study because it symbolizes the clerical state. Unlike their Protestant counterparts, Catholic women pastors are also prohibited from wearing a chasuble or a stole. The chasuble is a sleeveless outer vestment worn by the officiating priest during Mass, and the stole is a vestment consisting of a long cloth band worn traditionally around the neck, like a scarf hanging down in front, by bishops and priests, and over the left shoulder by deacons.

However, there were two or three dioceses I visited where the guidelines require that pastoral administrators wear an alb at all ceremonial functions. The alb, a full-length white linen vestment with long sleeves gathered at the waist with a cincture, and worn during Mass by priests under the chasuble, was described in the previous chapter. As one of the lay pastors explained to me, the diocese views the alb as the dress of the layperson, and the stole, described above, designates ordination. In fact, I was told that there are some parishes where the eucharistic ministers [the parishioners who help to distribute Communion] also wear some sort of vestment. Therefore, if the altar servers, the priest, and the eucharistic ministers are all wearing vestments, then the woman pastor would look "out of place" on the altar without an alb.

In four of the twenty parishes I visited, the women pastors regularly wore an alb while on the altar during liturgical ceremonies. Many of those who wore lay clothes on these occasions, married women and nuns alike, argued vehemently against ever accepting any of the "clerical trappings," like a collar, chasuble, stole, or even an alb, because they identify very strongly with the laity, as the following statement from a married woman pastor illustrates:

> I dress in liturgical colors. In other words, if I am preaching during Advent, I wear a purple dress. My whole message to everyone in this parish is that I am a layperson and they are lay people. We had a group of people here who wanted me to wear an alb, and I said that just separates me from the people. I am just not into clerical dress.

Some of the nun pastors were equally vehement, for example, one of them explained:

> Even in the first pamphlet they gave us on what a pastoral administrator is supposed to be, they said that for the Communion services or the Sunday liturgies we were supposed to

wear an alb. But the albs that were here were extremely long. I thought I wasn't going to spend that much money for that. My whole thinking was: "I am part of the people; we are the church." So there was no need to be dressing any special way because I am one of them. I don't want to be different. I don't want to pull myself away from them; I want to be with them.

Another woman pastor who wore only lay clothes in her parish said that perhaps if she went to another parish, she might wear something symbolic. However, she was undecided about wearing liturgical garb, and she explained,

I go back and forth because, on the one hand, there is something about having them say, as they do to me, "You're one of us," in looking like that. There is something about that that is very precious and I don't want that to be erased because I am wearing liturgical garb. On the other hand, I have done some reading and heard some people talk about the importance of the presider's role and the liturgical vestment, and I do key into that, too. So I don't know. I'm back and forth on that.

Do women who are members of religious communities, who have the title "Sister," and who may wear clothing symbolic of their religious state, experience an easier acceptance by the parishioners than married women or single women who are not nuns?

This question, of course, is difficult to answer for a number of reasons. First of all, I found that the title "Sister" does not lessen the resistance of some parishioners who are distrustful of outsiders in general. For instance, in a rural parish where the nun pastor was from a large city, the sacramental minister said,

I believe when a priest walks into a parish, they are immediately accepted. It's just a strong tradition and no questions are asked. And there's kind of a sense of, "We know who he is because he's wearing a Roman collar." But I would say when [the nun pastor] arrived here, because she was a woman, and because she was [from a large city], there was a lot of skepticism, and people were going to kind of step back and wait and see who this newfangled minister was in town. So she didn't get the immediate reception that I think a priest would.

On the other hand, a woman parishioner who described herself to me as a conservative Catholic had this to say:

The shock was very hard for people to handle, that it was just done so fast. And certainly from my point of view, I was happy we were getting a sister rather than a "layperson." I know nuns are officially "lay," but nonetheless it's a committed, dedicated religious life. That distinction is very important to me personally, so I've always felt we were very lucky to have a nun heading the parish.

Since Vatican II most nuns have adopted the clothing of the laity, so they no longer "stand out in a crowd" as do priests wearing clerical collars. In fact, in only one of the eleven parishes run by nuns did I see a woman pastor wear anything that resembles a religious habit. In this case she wore lay clothes most of the time, but she donned a "modified habit," consisting of a blue street-length dress with a small blue veil on her head for Sunday services. Several of the woman pastors, nuns and married women alike, wore a small cross during the Sunday liturgies. In fact, the cross worn by the woman pastor in two of the parishes I visited was given to her by the parishioners.

CONFLICTS AND TENSIONS IN DAILY ENCOUNTERS

As might be expected, bishops, priests, parishioners, and women pastors did not always agree about the constraints of the institutional church. Some held more traditional positions, and some less so. These differences, in turn, often caused conflicts in daily encounters, and increased the tension as they attempted to work together in the parish.

These kinds of encounters, critical to the woman's success as a pastor, could never be adequately understood by analyzing responses to a written survey. They can, however, be examined by interviews with the principal informants and by observations in natural settings. Because an understanding of both the supports and constraints involved in the everyday activities of women pastors was my chief goal in undertaking this project, my research design included both depth interviewing and participant observation.[3] Another source of knowledge about these everyday encounters, of course, would be autobiographical accounts of the principal informants. To this end I have been and continue to encourage women pastors to keep a journal and eventually write of their experiences in order to expand our understanding of this phenomenon.

Woman Pastor and Priest

In looking at the consequences of institutional constraints on the role of a woman pastor in everyday encounters, I will focus first on the relationship between her and the priest assigned as the sacramental minister. This is a sensitive relationship, because the pastor must depend on him to perform ritual activities central to the pastoral role. The moments of his interventions are, therefore, illustrative of the restrictions on her power in the parish.

Typically, the sacramental minister travels from his own parish on the weekend to preside at the Mass, and often he would leave immediately afterward. The role of the pastor during the Sunday Mass was more restricted in some parishes than others. As a male parishioner described it:

> There are several priests that come here who will not allow her on the altar with them, and that's a bone of contention with the parishioners, because she is our pastoral director. She is our spiritual leader at this point, the person we go to when we need advice and help and leadership. I feel uncomfortable with the fact that she cannot be part of the service.

A female parishioner in the same parish said,

> Everybody mentions that we would like to see her be more a part of the Mass. That seems to be a constant topic of conversation, I would say especially from the women. But also some of the men feel like [her] role in this whole thing is very spiritual, and sometimes she gets lost in the administrative end.

In general, much of the conflict between pastor and sacramental minister was related to different expectations about how this new role was to be acted out in the parish. One of the women pastors said:

> For me, the constraints continue to be around the expectations of the ordained ministers. Their expectations and my expectations are really different, and their perception of what we are working toward does not always jibe. Sometimes it does intellectually, but I don't find the practices always working in the

same direction. I think the various expectations, and not being able to come to some "clicking" on those, continues to cause tension that is hard periodically, especially with certain things in the ministry that make it obvious. That is a constraint for me.

Several of the women I interviewed expressed their disappointment at not being encouraged to preach by the sacramental minister. One of the priests explained why he did not encourage the woman pastor to preach during the Sunday Mass. He said,

> For me the presider is to be the homilist. So I do not invite her to homilize as frequently, for example, as my predecessor did. I am more of a stickler on some liturgical things. One of the things I believe is that if I am presiding at the eucharist, then normally I should be the one who gives the homily. Now I am not a stickler in the sense that I would be hung up on it, and if she ever came and said, "I would really like to give some words on this at this Mass," I would say, "Great, go ahead."

Even the practice of a woman pastor presenting a summary of a priest's homily can be resisted by priests who object to a woman's presence in the sanctuary. The woman pastor in a Mexican-American parish said that among the priests who served her parish, there was only one who could speak Spanish, and he came only occasionally during the summer. She said,

> The others don't know Spanish, so after they finish the homily in English, I give the summary in Spanish. One [priest] told me it wasn't necessary, and I said it is necessary because there are some people who don't understand English.

Because he often serves two or more parishes, the role of the sacramental minister has its limitations as well. One of the women pastors said,

> I think we want to be very sensitive to the priests so they don't feel like they are somebody who just comes in here because we have to have this warm body, that they are valued, too, that they have something to give to our community. So that takes some balancing to work that out.

The "balancing" can be difficult. This is especially true in the typical situation where only one sacramental minister has been assigned to the parish. In these cases, the two must work out any conflicts between them, since there are no alternatives.

By contrast, a woman pastor in a diocese critically short of priests had no single priest assigned to her parish. Instead, the bishop gave her the task of locating the priests for the sacramental liturgies in her parish. She had this to say:

> I do have the choice of who comes for Mass. I make the arrangements; nobody else makes them for me. If I have somebody who is undercutting me, he doesn't come back. I had that happen my first three months here and he didn't come back. If somebody told me that this person was going to be my sacramental minister, I would fight that tooth and nail. I want to choose that. I will take the hassle of having to find priests any day over having somebody imposed on me.

Sometimes the priests who are substituting for the sacramental minister during his vacation have difficulties accepting the woman pastor as leader of the parish. A nun pastor described just such a situation.

> He didn't want me sitting next to him [on the altar] to begin with. I said, "This is what we do here." And I sat next to him. But he never looked at me. I was a nonperson. And those are the kinds of things where my frustration hits.

Some of the women resolve the conflict about their role with regard to the sacraments by taking a more active stance. Several of them reported having heard confessions informally, although they cannot validly give absolution. A married woman pastor explained:

> I have found when people are sick that they are really confessing a lot of the time. I had one person say to me, "I have told you, and God is listening, and that's enough." I agreed.

A nun pastor described her response when parishioners came to her for confessions. She said,

> We were having a penitential service[4] and this person came to me and said, "Sister, could I talk with you?" I told him, "Yes, you can." So right there he started to talk, pouring out the whole thing. When he finished I told him, "Why don't you go now to Father and he will bless you." He said, "Do you think I am going to repeat what I told you to that man?" I said, "He is representing Jesus. He is only going to confirm the blessing." He said, "No, I am not going to. Do you think my sins are for-

given?" I said, "Of course your sins are forgiven. If you want to go, go, and if not, don't go." When they ask me if they need the priest for confession I tell them no, they don't.

Only two women pastors reported that they presided alone at baptisms. One of them explained,

> One time when we had baptisms, the priest didn't come, so we had a Communion service and I baptized the baby. Later on the young mother told me, "Sister, I'm so glad you did it."

Although nonordained persons are not permitted to perform the sacrament of the anointing of the sick [often referred to as one of the "last sacraments"], it is often difficult to find a priest to officiate at the critical moment, and if they are not able to find a priest, some of the women pastors perform the rite themselves. In one parish the woman pastor told how she solved a dilemma for a dying woman who was in dreadful pain, but who, as her husband described it, was "holding on" for the sacrament of the anointing of the sick. After trying unsuccessfully to locate a priest, the woman pastor arrived at the hospital room, leaned down to speak into the ear of the dying woman, and, as she reported it:

> I made sure she knew who I was and what I was doing, and I said we would go through the whole rite just as if she had a priest. Her husband said that was what she wanted, and I wasn't gone ten minutes when she let go. And she was in terrible pain.

Although the woman pastor is also responsible for the preparations for the sacrament of confirmation, she does not expect to preside because this is typically the bishop's responsibility. However, even on these occasions there are tensions with the priest who is also present on the altar. A woman pastor described such a scene thus:

> So the bishop comes and they do their little thing. In the end Father is thanking everybody who helped, the musicians and everybody who helped. He didn't say my name. This was to the whole congregation. I could have just throttled him.

Another aspect of the conflicts between the woman pastor and the sacramental minister is that he is often late, or fails to show up for the Sunday Mass at her parish. When the priest knows that he will consistently be late because of his schedule in other parishes, and it is impossible to change Mass schedules in the parishes, he may even work out a compromise with the woman pastor where she would "start" the Mass by presiding at the first part of the service consisting of the opening prayers and the liturgy of the word [scripture readings and homily]. As as soon as he arrived, he would "take over," because only a priest can preside for the second part, the liturgy of the eucharist [offertory, consecration, and Communion]. One sacramental minister described such a situation:

> Many times because of the schedule, they [the woman pastor and her congregation] would start and I would come in after the start. Many times I would leave before Communion would start because I would have another Mass to go to.

A similar incident was reported by a woman pastor who said,

> He was a prison chaplain and he got locked up...during a breakout, and he couldn't make Mass. We knew this was going to happen someday. It was on a Saturday and I had two hundred children in church. It was the kickoff Mass for the religious education program. I waited twenty minutes and the children became restless, so we started Mass without him. I figured he would get there sometime and if not, I would do a dry Mass,[5] that's all. And I explained this to the children. I was in the middle of the homily when he came racing down the aisle, and then afterwards he said, "I bet she was going to put on the vestments." And all the kids giggled.

Celebrating Mass as a "team" can be an awkward situation, involving logistics that are both liturgically questionable and perhaps incomprehensible to the congregation. I should hasten to say that the above situations were reported to occur only rarely.

What was reported more frequently to me, however, was a real "no show" on the part of the priest, either because he misinterpreted the schedule, or because he was sick or was called out of town unexpectedly. In these cases, the woman pastor would announce the priest's absence to the congregation and explain that she would be presiding at a word and Communion service.

I was an observer in such a situation, and I noted that prior to the beginning of the service, the woman pastor asked if there were any visitors from out of town in the congregation. After a few people identified themselves as such, she then very carefully described a word and Communion service. After that she explained to those gathered in the church that the service to be performed, although strictly speaking would fulfill their Sunday obligation, it would not be a Mass, and she invited those who wanted to leave in order to attend Mass elsewhere to do so. No one left the church on that occasion, and from what I heard in the parishes I visited, only rarely did people ever leave; in most instances the entire congregation remained to participate in the word and Communion service.

When the priest's absence was unexpected, there is always the danger that there may not be an ample supply of consecrated hosts available. Such was the case in a situation described by a woman pastor:

> We had four hosts for 136 people. I turned and there were all these people and I had four hosts. They saw my face and they all looked and I said, "Let's pray for the multiplication of the loaves here." So we broke and broke and broke, and I told the people, "This is where I feel my poverty of the nonordained because there is a bowl of [unconsecrated] hosts in the sacristy." So I held up Jesus between my fingers and said, "Trust me, this is the Lamb of God." And everybody got a little piece.

As I explained in an earlier chapter, there are some parishes where the priest comes for Mass only twice a month, and in one or two parishes he appears only once a month. In these parishes the woman pastors regularly preside at word and Communion services on the weekend. A male parishioner reported that one of their former priests expressed his reservations about the word and Communion services at a parish meeting. As the parishioner described it,

> He was very threatened by the fact that we had women doing these services. Someone [a parishioner] said, "Well, Father, after people start seeing what's going on at the Communion services you may not have as many at your Mass." And it was almost as if somebody dropped a bomb.

The same parishioner continued with a reflection on the collaborative stance of the women who were presiding at these services:

It's ministry not by a person on a pedestal. It is out there at the level of the people, and the sisters are doing it and are not putting themselves on a pedestal. Sometimes priests tend to do that. So that was a power situation.

As we saw in chapter 4, where the collaborative leadership style of woman pastors was discussed, there is often a stark contrast between the extent of parishioner participation in parish activities before and after her arrival. However, there are some situations where the sacramental minister is not in agreement with this new direction. One of the women pastors complained about this when she said,

I really don't think I am free to pursue what I believe needs to be done in order to prepare the people. And I don't think that the priest I am working with has the same vision of empowerment of lay people. He can say all the right words, but at the gut level he doesn't allow it to happen.

At the heart of the tensions involved in the encounters between woman pastor and sacramental minister is the question of power. As a priest-pastor in his own parish he traditionally had [and may still have] virtually unlimited power. And his travels to her parish are for the specific purpose of fulfilling functions that are beyond the limits of her authority. He has a "piece of the pie," so to speak, in her parish. What does this look like from the priest's vantage point? One of the sacramental ministers explained,

I find among the priests, as a whole, just a general acceptance of them [woman pastors] and the situation. Everyone knows it is going to happen. Now there is a lot of comparison [of woman pastors] that happens, and a lot of it has to do with—and this is priest talk—"She'd really want to be a priest." And so if there is some sense that they are intruding in our space, then I think that causes tension. There was a situation in this deanery that was difficult because the priest felt his space was being [intruded]; he was being told what to do [by the woman pastor] in an inappropriate manner.

On the other hand, every time the sacramental minister arrives at her parish to fulfill his sacramental functions, in a sense he is invading the woman pastor's "turf," because she has overall responsibility for the parish. And since he is accustomed to being the authority figure, it may be very difficult for him not to revert back to "putting himself on a pedestal," expecting the people to come to him, and "taking over."

Some of the priests did take over in the sense of limiting the woman pastor's opportunities for preaching, for example. But not one of the sacramental ministers was seen as trying to move her out of her position and take it over himself. Most of the priests were overburdened, in fact some were already suffering from burnout, and had neither the time nor the energy to take on another parish.

Pastor and Parishioners

One of the first obstacles the woman pastor meets on her arrival is a reluctance on the part of the parishioners to accept her as their leader. One of the female parishioners attributed this reluctance to the the parishioners' attitudes regarding the traditional authority of the priest. She said,

> Her predecessor had Divine Rule because he was a priest, and what he said was readily accepted as God's law. I think what Sister says isn't quite accepted, but she's willing to discuss it with the parishioners, to make the parishioners part of as many decisions as she possibly can.

Parishioners' views regarding priestly power was also mentioned by a married woman pastor when she recounted her confrontation with the parish finance council. She said,

> We were doing the budget. I said I really needed a secretary. I said I have a typewriter and phone at home, but I don't have the time when I'm home, and I really felt a need for a secretary, probably eight hours a week. I approached the finance council about it, and they said they would talk to the parish council. So they talked to the parish council, and the parish council bounced it back to the finance council. I went to the finance council meeting and said, "Hey, guys, if somebody with a Roman collar said, 'I want a secretary,' you would say, 'Yes, Father.' I am telling you we are having a secretary." And that was the end of it.

Another married woman pastor, who said that some of her parishioners were constantly asking the sacramental minister to perform various functions for them, decried the fact that she needed to clarify publicly again and again precisely what the duties of the sacramental minister were. She said, "That's one of the things I don't think we will ever get over as long as we don't wear the Roman collar."

Some of the conflict between a woman pastor and her parishioners revolves around her role as presider at word and Communion services. Older and more conservative Catholics are especially bothered by the sight of a woman leading the services at the altar. A male parishioner explained,

> The first three months were very hard on [her], and were hard on a lot of us, too, because we were not well prepared. There was a fair amount of resistance, and quite a bit of initial change, especially going from Mass to Communion service, and some of these kinds of things. The parish suffered maybe a little bit in those few months, and I know [she] suffered a lot.

One of the female parishioners compared her change of attitude with that of others in the parish when she said,

> It really doesn't bother me as much as I thought it was going to. The sisters have done such a good job with the eucharistic service, I am not missing the consecration part of the Mass, and we have everything else. So it really hasn't bothered me. Some people it has; it depends on who you are going to talk to. There are going to be a few who don't accept the fact that sisters can do it. But I think they are effective, and it doesn't bother me that I don't go to Mass, because they do such a good job with their services. And we've had better sermons from them than we have had from some of the priests we've had.

The church's position regarding the right of a layperson to preach the homily during Mass, for instance, inspires many different interpretations, and thus creates some controversies. A woman pastor described such a conflict situation in her parish.

> Last year there was an uprising because I was doing the homily, and there was an article in the [diocesan newspaper] that stated that women shouldn't be doing the homilies. And before you knew it, there was this whole ferment going on in

the parish. I knew who the people were, and they had given me a problem ever since I came here. They don't like the changes and would like to see me out. So I said to [the sacramental minister], "I think the only way to handle this is to confront it face on."

She explained how the priest took the occasion to raise the issue while she was on vacation:

He did it during the homily. He kind of used the scriptures of the day and then went into [explaining] we're all family and how we support one another. Then he went into the fact that there had been some rumblings about my doing the homily, and he said how he suggested it right from the very beginning, and how the bishop knew about it, and how I had given homilies that are much better than some of the priests that he knows. I mean he just laid it on the line. That was very important.

In this instance, the priest took the responsibility for authorizing her to preach during Mass, and added further legitimacy to her actions by arguing that the bishop was aware of the situation.

PERSONAL CONCERNS AND TENSIONS

In the previous chapter we concentrated on the bright side of the coin, the supports and resources available to women pastors, but, as we have seen, this chapter looks at the flip side. In order to have a more complete understanding of that "dark side" of the role of a woman pastor we will now look at those personal concerns and tensions that are in part a consequence of the institutional constraints and the conflicts she experiences in her relationships between herself and the other key individuals, that is, the parishioners, priests, and bishop. The question we are raising here is, "What do these key individuals think about the limitations of this new role, and what are their feelings about it?"

One of the priests whom I interviewed spoke about the "whole liturgical tension of what their [the women pastors'] role really is." For example, he cited baptisms that are done during Mass, and asked what is appropriate for women pastors to do. As he said,

We are really trying to give them everything that they can do that is appropriate, or maybe even stretching the appropriateness canonically. So they [women] lead the community in the renewal of baptismal promises and do the giving of the candle and the garment, and basically we [priests] do the anointing and the pouring of water.

A nun pastor expressed very strong feelings about her lack of credentials when she said,

This is the first time in any ministry I have been in where I have not had the credentials to do what I am asked to do. When I taught, I was certified to teach, and when I worked in the retreat apostolate I was certified as a spiritual director. But now we are asked by [the bishop] to pastor these parishes and to be the spiritual person to lead them, and we can only do so much, and then we have to put the skids on. We can't give absolution, though we hear confessions all the time down in the parlor. We can't anoint when we go to the hospital, though we bless them. They ask, "Is this going to be okay now, Sister?" I say, "Yes, it is. I am sure God has forgiven you. Father will be in to give you the blessing of the church."

Another nun pastor used the analogy of trying to dig a hole without tools. She said,

The most difficult moments were helping persons get ready for the sacraments and not being able to celebrate the sacraments with them. The image that comes to my mind is: you give someone a job...for instance, "You need to dig this hole here, but I tie your hands, so do it." Or, "The tools are there, but you cannot touch them." I really think that deep down I am called to minister. That is why sometimes it makes me feel so bad that they give me a job and then they tie my hands up.

On the other hand, how do sacramental ministers feel about their role, particularly those who minister in two or more parishes? A young priest who was reflecting on his role as sacramental minister to three parishes said that he felt he was becoming a sort of "sacramental parachuting priest," and this discouraged him. Another sacramental minister said that the woman pastor did all of the preparations for the sacraments in the parish, and his role, as he described it, was to "come swooping in from heaven and lay on the appropriate magic." A third sacramental minister who had a full-time job teaching at the local seminary, and who did not have his own parish, expressed his reservations in this way:

> I have on occasion found it very difficult to come and do the sacramental thing, and then leave. We were joking in the diocese once that I was the sacramental stud. I'd just go and do my thing, and that's it. I don't think that that can work, and so that's a real concern I have about this whole direction.

In this instance the priest was expressing a lack of connectedness, or anomie, as sociologists call it. Although in most cases the sacramental minister scarcely knew the parishioners, he had to be called in to perform their baptisms, marriages, and the final anointings at their deaths. The women pastors who are responsible for preparing their parishioners for these occasions reported that the greatest point of tension is here, at the moment when they must place themselves "in the back of the church," as it were, and let the "real priest" take over. A nun pastor said:

> I would like to get more involved in the sacraments because I do the preparations for baptism and I'm not able to do anything in the actual baptism. The sick—we have a little boy here who is nine years old who is dying of leukemia, and I spent literally my first two years here in and out with the family, hours and hours. And then when it comes to the funeral, well I did the homily for that, so I did feel that I was part of it. But very often I almost feel as though I am on the outskirts of it, and I mind that.

She continued,

> I don't even like to think about it too much because I get feeling a little like, "This is really dumb." I try not to think about it too much. Like the sacrament of reconciliation [confession], for instance, I prepare those kids for the sacrament. One of the kids came up to me one day and said, "Why can't I go to you for confession? I'd rather go to you." And I know some of the couples, too, they really want me to be there and want to make sure I am going to be at the wedding or reception. I guess they know very well that I can't do much more. Deep down I wish it would change.

She summed it up by saying that she felt "kind of on the fringe" when it comes to the sacraments. Terms like "on the outskirts," "on the fringe," and "feeling like a nonperson," kept emerging when the woman pastors discussed their role in the sacraments.

A married woman pastor who had talked about it with her priest, reported,

> He tells me that part of my frustrations is that I am doing all this work and I can't actually do the sacrament. And I told him, "No, it's there. I realize it and know I can't do it, but it's a loneliness or an emptiness I can live with because I know right now I can't do anything about it."

The same woman talked about feeling like a nonperson because she was "not in the picture":

> You know, afterwards they take pictures of the baptism group with Father. And I'm not in the picture.

One of the women pastors explained how she felt when the priest she located for the anointing of the sick was someone who did not know the family.

> If it's a priest who knows them, I feel a little bit more comfortable. If it is [a situation where I] call the chancery and just a hot body with a Roman collar shows up, it really hurts. And I think it hurts more so because of the family who may be standing around the bed, knowing that this stranger is going to say some prayers for somebody they love very dearly. And, if it is somebody who is that kind of person, they normally do not ask me to participate, and I think it hurts the families more than it hurts me.

The parishioners, who observed the subservient role of the woman pastors on these occasions, also expressed their disappointment. A female parishioner, for example, said,

> I don't think that it's fair to [the lay pastor]. I can't think of a comparison, but it just doesn't seem like [lay pastors] should have all the work and not reap the final benefit. To me it's the most gratifying to actually perform the marriage and to actually do the baptism. That's where the real gratification comes in, so it is like they are doing all the work and they don't get to sit down and reap the rewards.

The parishioner quoted above stopped me the day after our interview to tell me that she had finally thought of a comparison

regarding the sacramental limitations of lay pastors. She presented the situation where someone performs all of the preparations
for a dinner, and then must leave the room when the guests
arrive and let someone else take over, thus forgoing the gratifica-
tions of eating the food and enjoying the company of the guests.

A parishioner in another parish who served as the organist
and choir director said,

> I resent it more and more because [the woman pastor] does
> such a beautiful job. She has done all the footwork. She's done
> everything. I just feel so frustrated for her because I just know
> how I would feel if I prepared all the music, did all the plan-
> ning, practiced [with] the folks, and somebody else came in
> and played the organ and directed, and I sat on the side and
> watched the whole thing happen.

Some of the priests were sensitive to the pain experienced
by woman pastors over the inequity of the sacramental situation.
A woman pastor described how a priest explained it to the congregation from the pulpit:

> At a wedding [the sacramental minister] said, "I think you all
> need to know that Sister _____ is the one who has walked
> with this couple all these months, and in some way it hurts—
> when the big day comes, she steps aside."

There is no doubt that the central concern and the point of
greatest tension for women pastors is that they cannot totally minister to their parishioners. Using the analogy of the shepherd, they
can watch over their flock, but they must call on someone else to
feed them. And it is this incompleteness—or emptiness, as one of
the women pastors put it—that is at the heart of their tensions.

But their limited empowerment is not the only issue that
causes strain. Finances are also a concern for all of the women
pastors. As we saw earlier, the compensation they receive is
minimal, at best. One might argue that nuns are accustomed to
receiving low wages, and they have a vow of poverty, so the
salary should be sufficient for them. On the contrary, most of the
sisters I spoke with were very concerned about their compensation because such a large percentage of the members of their
religious communities were elderly, and needed their financial
support. One of the nun pastors said,

It would be hard for me to ask for a better compensation, and yet I do support that, and I do get my word in because every one of us who is a working religious in our community supports two sisters who are retired. That's the state of every congregation.

What the nuns told me was that their salaries as pastoral administrators were much lower than what they could earn as teachers in a public school system, for instance. Nonetheless, their religious communities were willing to allow them to work for the lower compensation in a parish for a time, because their work in the parish was defined by the sisters as dedicated service to the church. However, the burden of supporting the retired sisters would force the community eventually to ask the women pastors to leave their present positions, unless their compensation could be increased.

The lay pastors, married and single, likewise suffer from the financial constraints of a low salary. Although all of the husbands are working full-time or are drawing retirement pensions, the married pastors have families to support, as do the nuns, who have the responsibility of supporting their religious community. An additional concern of some of the women pastors whom I interviewed was that they were working with overdue contracts; in fact, one of them was still operating without a written contract.

In general, finances are a major problem in poor parishes, and this is the case for the vast majority of the parishes I visited. The Sunday collection, for instance, is usually insufficient to cover any renovation expenses for the parish buildings. Fundraising events like annual bazaars and quilting sales are a necessity in most of these parishes. In a parish with a high rate of unemployment a nun pastor told me that she obtained some much needed funds by speaking about the pressing needs of her parish at all of the Masses one weekend at a wealthy parish in her diocese. Although she did not enjoy her "begging expedition," she felt she had no other alternative, and it enabled the parish to pay its bills.

Another cost for some of them is travel time. Women pastors who live in isolated areas, and who are in charge of more than one parish, share a deep concern about the time and energy they must expend traveling from parish to parish. As I accompanied them on their travels, I realized that an inordinate amount of their time was spent in the car. One of the nuns who was copastoring with a member of her religious community calculated that they put in about two thousand miles a month traveling from parish to parish. She said,

> We get very drained because we have a hard time getting the time we need for ourselves, with that kind of mileage. When we talk about a day off, we are talking about not a day off, but about doing all of the house-oriented kinds of things that have to get done, as any working person has to experience.

As I mentioned earlier, another concern for some of the women pastors is their living situation. The five women who live alone in their parish houses said that they did not mind living alone because they were so busy throughout the day, and gone so much, that they appreciated the quiet and space when they came home. Ideally, though, they would like to have someone living with them to share their meals, their prayers, and their daily joys and sorrows. In addition, two of the married women living at their own homes with their families had to create an office in the home because the parish, which had only been in existence for a short time, owned neither a church building nor a pastor's office. These were parishes mentioned earlier that rented space from a local Protestant church for Sunday services. Both of the women pastors were very anxious to move the parish office out of their homes, because it occupied space needed by the family.

This completes our glimpse of the personal concerns and tensions surrounding the role of the woman pastor. This chapter examined the conflicts and tensions engendered by church teachings, laws, and practices that serve to cloud the role of the woman pastor in varying degrees of ambiguity and uncertainty. These conflicts and personal tensions are present in their interactions with priests and parishioners because women pastors are reminded on a daily basis that as laity—and especially as women—they are not fully pastors.

That these women pastors are on the "frontline," so to speak, in a movement toward an altering of the limited image of the "good woman," may be of little solace to them in their day-to-day experiences. But the significance of what they are doing in these parishes must not be underestimated. It is these issues that I will address in the next chapter on the "Woman Question."

•8•

Gender and the Pastoral Role

The idea of a woman pastor is so incongruous for many Catholics that they can hardly imagine it. It is incompatible with their only image of a Catholic pastor: a priest, an ordained male, the dominant figure in the parish, whose parishioners traditionally both revere and obey him. A woman in charge of a parish does not look like a pastor, she does not sound like a pastor, and she does not act like most previous pastors.

How, then, do people react to a person in a new position like this, who is not of the "appropriate" gender? And how do women in this new position meet the challenges to an effective performance of their responsibilities?

These two major parts of the "woman question" are not unique to women pastors. They can be applied, in fact, to all women who are moving into occupations that were formerly reserved solely for males. How can this be so? It could be argued that most women in male-dominated jobs have challenges, but at least they have the law on their side. That is, there are no laws on the books that exclude women from jobs that were formerly male-dominated positions such as senators, Supreme Court justices, governors, mayors, military officers, corporate executive officers, construction supervisors, and university presidents. Women in these positions may not have an easy time of it, but they have no *de jure* constraints, as do the women pastors.

The *de jure* constraint, which prohibits women from ordination, still exists and is well known to all, clergy and laity alike.

Therefore, women in charge of parishes are aware of the constraints placed on them because of their gender. In fact, they were cognizant of their limited empowerment well before they arrived at the parish. Because they share their status as laity with their parishioners, they bring a different perspective to their ministry. As we saw in chapters 3 through 5, her experience as a layperson enables her to exercise collaborative, rather than hierarchical, leadership. Her experience as a laywoman is also the impetus for her attempts at restructuring her parish and for her efforts to forge a bond with her parishioners.

A nun pastor remarked that laity have been treated "as peasants" in the church, and she shares that aspect of her history as a Catholic with them. On the other hand, women as mothers have an exalted position in the Catholic church, as is evident in the devotion to the Blessed Virgin Mary over many centuries. But women in that honored position do not exercise any power beyond the confines of their homes; in fact, relegating women to the private sphere of the home reinforces their low status in the public sphere of the "real world." Thus laywomen belong on the lowest rung of the "peasantry" in the church, and, as in a caste system, their low status in the church was determined at birth and is presumably lifelong.

It is no wonder then, that the first few women appointed to head parishes became celebrities almost overnight. A few of them have been on television talk shows, and one of them who was featured in a special report on national television told me that the television crew spent a week doing the filming and interviewing in her parish. One of the women pastors showed me a large album filled with newspaper articles, pictures, and letters, and she described her reactions in this way:

> It was in the diocesan paper, the local paper, and the [metropolitan area] paper. All of a sudden I was a celebrity. It was unnerving in some ways because I began getting all of these cards and letters of congratulations. Of course, what I loved was that many of them were from women.

Women who are the "firsts" to move into positions previously held by men in secular institutions and organizations also experience the "instant celebrity" syndrome. However, unlike their counterparts heading Catholic parishes, they have no *de jure* obstacles. Nonetheless, they often find that there are a number of *de facto* constraints once they appear on the scene at their new job locations. And, in fact, these constraints may be more difficult to deal with, because they are often unwritten, almost always unexpected, and seldom acknowledged by the people with whom they are working.[1]

In the last analysis, what all women in formerly male-only occupations have in common is that some of the people with whom they must interact on their jobs may not welcome them. Such persons may, in fact, deter them in their daily encounters, primarily because of ingrained and long-held biases regarding a "woman's place" and limited capabilities, which lead to an uncomfortable clash of expectations with realities in these situations.[2]

In this chapter, as we focus on the woman question, we examine three of its components in the daily lives of woman pastors: patriarchy, gender discrimination, and progress toward nonsexist attitudes and actions.

PATRIARCHY AND GENDER INEQUALITY

The Catholic church as an institution is the personification of a hierarchical system based on patriarchy, where men who are considered superior hold all the positions of power. A belief in patriarchy guarantees a dominant position for males because the primacy of their authority is unquestioned. The use of terms like "your eminence" and "your excellency" reserved for cardinals and bishops, all of whom are men, is a case in point.

I found that the belief that men should rule was played out in numerous ways in the everyday lives of women pastors. It was particularly evident in the way some of the sacramental ministers related to them. As a nun pastor described it,

> At the beginning I was told I couldn't preach. He [the sacramental minister] talked about it and told me what I could do and what I couldn't do. He is a very dominating person. He's a good person and he would like to think that he is very supportive of me in leadership roles. But on the other hand, if I were to say something about "my parish," which I have, but I don't do it anymore; I never meant it as mine. But when I

would say, "out at my parish," he would say, "It's 'our.'" So I got used to that.

The same woman explained that this priest made it clear to her that he wanted to do things "his way," so she had to be tactful about making any suggestions or recommendations to him. As she described it:

> To put it most simply, I feel tired if I have to work at being diplomatic with [him], and make a suggestion and make it sound like he made it in order to make it work out right. And sometimes that wearies me.

A similar situation can emerge in the relationships between women pastors and male parishioners. A young married woman told of the conflict she had with a very domineering male parishioner, a leader of the parish, who was a member of the parish council. She said,

> I think the guy has a real problem with women in authority, no matter what. And as long as I would kiss up to him and let him have the upper hand, it was okay. One day I didn't do that, and he just blew up.

A middle-aged woman pastor encountered the same difficulty. She stated,

> There were people who had a very difficult time accepting a woman. It is an Hispanic parish, and we do have the macho Mexican there. I still am fighting with a couple of people where I have had to come down very authoritarian a couple of times, and I don't like to do that. That's not my style, but the only way I can get my point across sometimes is to say, "I'm the boss; you do it my way."

A similar statement came from a woman pastor in a predominantly white parish:

> Probably the main problem I had was being a female in a leadership role in a mining town that's very macho. I was very cautious in the demands that were made in the parish for the first year.

Likewise, a nun pastor described what ensued immediately after she stood up to a male parishioner at a parish council meeting.

Four of them [parish council members] stayed with me an hour after that, supporting me basically, because they said, "He had done this before; he's always ruled the roost." He had done it with the priests as well. So I didn't know what was going to happen. I certainly didn't want to cause a major eruption, but I wasn't going to let this man rule me for the whole time I was here. And the whole first year had been a real struggle with him. I tried to be gentle with him, but firm, listen to him, but he was totally disrespectful. He had no respect for me. It was really a woman issue. He is really a male chauvinist to the teeth.

A female parishioner said that there was a lot of "hell raising" when the parishioners heard that "a woman was going to be boss." She quoted one of the women of the parish who told her,

> I know these men. They don't want a woman in charge. They think all we are good for is cooking in the kitchen, and making love, and having babies. We're going to show them.

Often I would hear my interviewees allude to the root of patriarchal attitudes and actions among Catholics, the stance of the institutional church. A male parishioner who was critical of the gender inequality in the church said,

> I would like to see more liberal views towards women as far as active roles in the church because they are a valuable resource. I think we have done a disservice, especially to some of the sisters who have devoted their lives the same as a priest has. Why should they be treated different? Just because they are female doesn't mean they are not capable of the same feelings, the same actions, everything. They are no different. The hierarchy is totally male, so it is hard for them to accept that.

A married woman pastor stated:

> It's just not right for the hierarchy to say to this group of people [women pastors], "No, you can't have complete and full action and movement in the sacraments, but only as we can dole it out to you according to some man, and [depending on] when he can come in here [to the parish]."

A nun pastor reported her perception of her bishop's reactions to the way she relates to him:

Probably he didn't expect my behavior to be what he has found. Probably he expected I was going to be like a little girl following orders, or something like that. And when he realized it was a woman who could confront him, I don't think he liked that too well because even his own priests don't speak to him like I do. There are some who disagree strongly with him, but I don't think he finds too much of that. Most of the priests who don't agree with him keep quiet.

This woman has no aspirations to membership in the hierarchy of the church, and indeed has no realistic grounds for such aspirations because as a woman she is destined to lifelong membership in the laity. In contrast to the priests who "keep quiet," she cannot identify with the hierarchy or aspire to any role within it. Thus she is free to confront the bishop since, in the last analysis, she has nothing to lose because she is not as closely connected to the diocese as priests are.

In a very straightforward statement about the consequences of working for a patriarchal church, a married woman pastor said,

I think it's the frustration of working on trying to break into the political system of the Catholic male church. I live in a relationship with the other half of mankind, my husband. We are equal. Somewhere around the tenth year [of our marriage] it was either we had this equality or we couldn't have a marriage, and we are happier. Our family's happier because of it, and it's very frustrating to go from that kind of a setting into the direct opposite. It frustrates me, and it doesn't make working there [in the parish] very joyful.

Prejudicial attitudes regarding gender based on centuries of patriarchal church tradition and practice clearly reveal themselves in many ways, as the above examples indicate.

GENDER DISCRIMINATION AND RESPONSES

In the case of a woman pastor, a belief in patriarchy on the part of bishops, priests, and parishioners often results in active discrimination against her. Reflecting on the source of gender discrimination, a married woman pastor said,

In all of the years of [my] gradually doing different things here, sitting on the council, being president of the council, leading prayer services, and all the other things, there was never any time where somebody said, "Wait a minute, [she] can't do that because she's a woman." It's only when you get into the areas of the Sunday Assembly, and then the actual, heavy-duty sacramental things, that the issue begins to surface. And it always comes from the top down, from the hierarchy. It's a problem for the hierarchy; it isn't a problem for the average people. And those people that do suffer from it and say, "Wait a minute, she's a woman," they didn't learn that themselves. It was taught to them, and they can learn to get past that, just as they can learn to get past judging a person because they are black or Mexican or Oriental, or any of the other things that they feel that puts constraints on them.

Some of the women pastors reported that they were often treated as if they were invisible when they attended meetings of the clergy. One of them spoke of feeling intimidated when she was the only woman among many priests wearing Roman collars, and another described a priest who kept his eyes down and would not look at her during a meeting. On the occasion of a Mass at the cathedral attended by all pastors, a woman pastor described how she and the only other woman pastor were treated:

Before the ceremony began, all the priests and the altar servers, and [the other woman pastor] and I were in the sacristy getting ready. We didn't wear albs. I'm sure I had a suit on. We processed in with them [the priests], and we bowed and went to our places in the sanctuary. But before we did that, in the sacristy when Father _____ and [she] and I were in conversation, the bishop came over and greeted Father and totally ignored [her] and myself. It was as if we weren't there. It was deliberate. And I knew it was deliberate because then five minutes later he crossed right in front of us again to greet the altar boys. As he crossed over, I was watching him just to see if he was going to say hello to us, and he caught my eye and put his eyes down, so I knew. And then at the end of Mass the bishop thanked everybody in the cathedral, from the choir through the people who set up the sacristy, for all their help, but he never acknowledged our presence. We went to the luncheon after, and he was there and he never talked to us there.

This woman expressed great anger at the way she had been treated by the bishop. She was equally critical of the first draft of the pastoral letter of the American bishops on women's concerns, which she analyzed as a statement of principles with no follow-up, that is, where they "say one thing and do another."

In an earlier chapter I described a decision of a bishop to ordain the husband of a woman pastor as a deacon. Not only was this an application of a law that directly discriminates against women because it states that only men may be ordained to the diaconate, but the bishop's decision was bound to cause tension in their copastoring situation. The woman in question explained her feelings about it when she said,

> I am happy for him [her husband], but I am sad for me. I don't think it's fair. It's really hard, that we have been doing this equally together for so long, and now he is going to be ordained and I am not. But that's reality, and you don't right a wrong by another wrong, like saying to somebody who has a vocation that they can't have it just because it's unfair to me. That's not how you right a wrong. So I have mixed feelings.

Several of the women pastors described how difficult it was for them to interact with priests when they were the only non-priest in attendance at meetings held specifically for pastors of the diocese. One of them had the following experience:

> The very first time I went to a meeting [for pastors] was at one of the staid parishes down in the center of town. I had received a letter about it, and they told me over the phone that the lunch would be at 12:30, followed by the meeting. Somehow or other it was at 12:00, but I didn't know that. So I arrived at the door, and when I told [the housekeeper] who I was, she said, "You're a nun?" I said, "Yes." She said, "Why aren't you wearing a habit?" Well, she was an older woman, and I came so close to saying, "None of your business, sweetie." I just let it go.
>
> She took me to the dining room and they [the priests] were a good way through the meal. I picked up a plate, and when I walked into the room—I always think of when a conductor gives a signal to an orchestra to stop—*everything stopped*. I didn't say anything. I was a little surprised because I wasn't expecting that, and I think they were surprised, too.

They knew who I was, but they didn't quite know what to do with me.[3] I thought to myself, "I'm going to wait until one of them says something." So I looked around for a chair, and there was no place at the table. But somebody got up right away and he said, "Sister, why don't you take my place because I am finished." I thanked him and took his place. Some people just said, "Nice to have you with us, Sister," and they broke the ice. And then it was all right.

Her words, "everything stopped," and "they didn't quite know what to do with me" point up the awkwardness for both the "only woman" and for the men in such a situation. Priest-pastors are obviously not accustomed to dealing with women as colleagues; their training leaves them ill-equipped for this type of an encounter. A woman pastor who had reflected on this lacuna in priest's lives made it a priority to attend each meeting or "study day" for pastors to which she was invited. She explained,

I will go to the study days because the priests need to see women there. It is important for the priests to talk to me in a nonthreatening atmosphere because some of them are going to be dealing with people like me in the next few years more and more. And they need to begin to realize that we don't bite.

On the other hand, one of the women pastors pointed out to me that meetings with priests can also silence the women attending. She was initially enthusiastic about attending meetings to which both women pastors and their sacramental ministers were invited. She soon lost her enthusiasm, because, as she put it,

We noticed that the men were dominating. So last September we all got together and at that meeting we told the sacramental ministers that as much as we [the women pastors] appreciated them, we thought we needed just to be with us, that they tended to dominate, and we needed things that were just appropriate for us. And that worked.

Another aspect of overt gender discrimination is exclusion. This usually takes the form of not receiving invitations to meetings for pastors of the diocese. Several of the women mentioned their disappointment at being excluded from some of these meetings. In one instance I was told that there was a diocesan meeting devoted solely to a discussion of alternate staffing of parishes to which no women pastors were invited. It would seem logical to include those with the most expertise on the topic among those invited, but such was not the case.

Parishioners as well as priests overtly expressed their bias in regard to the presence of women pastors. A male parishioner explained,

> There is still a little bit of bias in people. It is not going to go away. It is unfortunate, but there is. And when people are seeing women taking the place of where they have been seeing a man in that position for, well, some of them for seventy or eighty years, it was difficult for some to accept. But generally everything worked out pretty well. There is still a small percentage, I would say less than ten percent, that are quite upset with the whole thing.

A woman pastor described her experience with parishioners who initially questioned the appropriateness of her preaching.

> The Sunday after I came, I preached to the people and told them what I was doing. They didn't all click on that. After I preached, several of them came and told me that I had no business preaching up there. But they've come a long way [since then].

A sacramental minister reported,

> There were some people who, I understand, left the parish and said they just had a difficult time with a woman. A lot of it, I think, centered around her preaching more than her presence here. People have adjusted to that over the years, but I used to watch the people [while she was preaching], and the men would look up at the ceiling, and the women would look sideways. So there was a struggle in that way.

A female parishioner who described herself as a conservative Catholic had this to say:

> I have heard adults tell me that kids say that a woman does not belong on the altar. I think there are a lot of people in this area that are threatened by changing female roles, and I think the threat goes very deep with them. By the way, I am not sure this is bad at all. There still is a certain security in raising boys and raising girls, and keeping sexes distinct. Homosexu-

ality really scares the [local] macho. They want their sons to hunt, and they want sex roles absolutely clear. They find the blurring of sex roles a threat to keeping their boys straight.

This same parishioner told me that it turns her off when her woman pastor mentions anything about the woman's movement, or quotes from people involved in the woman's movement. On the other hand, she thinks her woman pastor is wonderful, and she supports her one hundred percent.

The issue of "appropriate" behavior for the different sex roles came up in several of the interviews. For example, the question of whether or not to fire the housecleaner for the parish house was raised. A woman pastor described her response.

> I remember that [the woman who cleaned the house] came in tears after Father left and said to me, "I suppose now that Father's gone that they won't hire me anymore." She thought I was going to do the cleaning. I said, "That shouldn't make any difference. I am doing everything Father did. You can be sure as long as I'm here you are going to stay on." Then I heard comments from the people, "Now that Sister is hired she will have more time so she can do her own cleaning." That was all the more reason why I didn't. I said, "I really wasn't trained to do the work of a housecleaner. I know how to do it, but my work is not that. My work is ministry here, and if Father could have somebody, I don't see why there should be a difference and I can't have somebody." She [the housecleaner] stayed on then.

In a similar incident in another parish, the sacramental minister reported some of the initial negative responses on the part of the parishioners to the nun pastor. He said that one of the interesting things was the decision of the altar and rosary society that "they really didn't have to wash the linens any more because a nun would do it."

The attitude of the parishioners in the accounts above are classic examples of gender discrimination, and they also exemplify entrenched beliefs about "a woman's place." In spite of the fact that the woman pastor had a full-time job, and that all of the previous pastors had housecleaners, because she happened to be a woman, she was expected to work the "second shift."[4] In fact, eight of the ten women pastors I interviewed who lived at the parish house did their own housecleaning, some because of the impoverished state of the parish, and others because they said they preferred to do their own cleaning. But in each case it was their own decision or preference to do so.

Another example of the response to gender discrimination emerged when a woman pastor described her encounter with the diocesan school board representatives. The issue was the amount that the parish had been assessed for the support of the Catholic schools in the diocese. She was unsuccessful in her attempt to persuade the school board to decrease her parish assessment, and she reported,

> I knew there were other pastors who were upset about this, and I said, "I'm getting no place because I'm a woman, number one, and they aren't paying any attention to me." So what I did was I invited some of the pastors in the area to meet, and I got a very generous response from them.

She then gathered the priests for a meeting, and they submitted a recommendation to the priest's council to have regional meetings to study the issue of Catholic education. She was also given a reprieve on her parish assessment by the diocese in the form of a "donation" to help her parish to meet the assessment. This woman pastor was aware that her assertiveness might not be appreciated by diocesan administrators. She said,

> So what I've done is I've gathered the priests. That's why I said I might not be here next year. I don't know what they'll do, but I've gotten very good responses from the priests.

Aside from the abilities of some of the women pastors to transform negative situations based on gender inequality into positive outcomes for themselves and for their parishes, there are also some indications that the patriarchial basis of gender bias is moving toward identifiable changes in the direction of gender equality. These indications are reflected in the issues we take up next, nonsexist attitudes and actions.

PROGRESS TOWARD NONSEXIST ATTITUDES AND ACTIONS

What were some of the indications that patriarchal beliefs and gender discrimination were being replaced by positive feminist beliefs and gender equality in the parishes I visited? There were a number of occasions during my travels to these parishes when the question of inclusive language emerged, sometimes during our conversations, and other times when I observed it in action, usually during the liturgy. For example, I noticed in one parish that hymns on xeroxed sheets showed words like "his" and other exclusive language had been deleted, and more inclusive language was inserted. In another parish I noticed that when the priest gave the last blessing at Mass, instead of "Father, Son, and Holy Spirit," he said, "Creator, Redeemer, and Holy Spirit." On neither of these occasions did I witness an uprising or even a mild protest from the congregation.

As we might expect, the efforts of women pastors to promote the use of inclusive language were not always met with enthusiasm, and in particular by priests. A nun pastor talked about one particular Sunday when the gospel was "one of the worst in terms of lack of inclusive language." She then said,

> So I went over to the church and took a pencil, feeling very secure in doing this, and changed the language in the lectionary.[5] [The priest who was the sacramental minister] came about an hour early, and he said to me, "Now is there anything we want to go over about the liturgy?" I said, "Oh, by the way, we're into some very sexist language in this translation, so I penciled in some changes." And he looked at me. I said, "You don't mind, do you? I've done just a little bit of changes to make it more inclusive, nothing drastic. I didn't change the sentence structure or anything, but I put in 'everyone' rather than 'men.'" And I tried to do it tastefully because I hate it when it's overdone. I said to him, "Are you comfortable with that?" And he said, "No, I am sad to say I am not comfortable with that. Now, if you had changed a psalm or one of the epistles or an Old Testament reading, I wouldn't have had any problem with that. But somehow I am not ready to change the wording of the gospel reading."

Without telling him, she then went back and erased the changes, and he thanked her for it, explaining, "I'm just not ready for that yet." She said that since that episode she has noticed that priests would change the language in the prayers, and would never say "mankind" or other exclusive words when they recited prayers, but they tended not to change the language of the gospel.

As I explained in a previous chapter, there is a difference of opinion among women pastors about their role during Sunday Mass. One of the women who usually wore an alb and was seated in the sanctuary next to the priest during Mass argued that it was important for her to take a public position in that setting. She described a meeting with other women pastors who differed with her.

> They [other women pastors] said, "That's okay for you, because you can get up there. You are good at being in the front and all that." And I looked at them and I said, "But I think that's a qualification to be a pastoral administrator, that you can be public. Otherwise I don't think we are doing anything that we haven't done as parish workers. It's just the whole concept of moving women into equal positions. And I don't see that as a power play, but rather as justice.

She continued,

> One of my strong convictions is that I am not up there for [myself]. I feel a real call to leadership for women, and so when I am up there I am representing women moving with more recognition into leadership as far as we can stretch that. And unless we do that, we are always going to just stay kind of the helpers for the priests, and I don't believe in that. I think that is a scary thing to deal with.

Another woman pastor spoke about the way she was treated when she attended local deanery meetings, where she was the only woman among five pastors. She said,

> But none of them greet me like I am second class. They respect my opinion and they listen. It's not a "me" and "them" situation.

Perhaps the change in attitudes and actions that have resulted from a woman pastor's activities in a parish can best be summed up by a woman parishioner, the parish organist and choir director, who said,

> I have really come to believe that women can do the job, not as well, but *better*. And believe it or not, when [the woman pastor] first came here, I didn't even change the words in the

hymns. That was not an issue at all. So I've grown a lot in the last four years, and realize what women can do for this church, and the position that women are in presently. And I don't think it's right.

At the beginning of this chapter I posed the "woman question" in two parts: how people react to the woman pastor and how she creatively meets the challenges of her new role. As is evident in the previous statement, it is the parishioners who witness the whole gamut of challenges stemming from patriarchal beliefs and practices that the woman pastor meets in her daily encounters. And it is the parishioners who, as laity, can identify with her treatment as a "second-class" citizen and who can also rejoice when they witness occasions when justice replaces sexism in her life as pastor. Even those parishioners who described themselves as traditional Catholics told me that they had changed their attitudes and actions regarding women in the church as a result of their experiences with their woman pastor. In short, the overwhelming majority of the parishioners I interviewed no longer support patriarchy and gender discrimination, and they attribute their change of attitude to their woman pastor.

•9•

Final Observations

This book has examined the woman-as-Catholic-pastor phenomenon from various perspectives as it exists now, in its early stages. The women pastors I interviewed can be described as pioneers or trailblazers because they were among the first to take on this new role in the United States. Therefore, their experiences may help to pave the way for others who will follow in their footsteps.

Any attempt to characterize this chapter as a conventional "conclusion" is tempered by an undeniable acknowledgement that the central subject matter of this book is still very much in process. I am well aware from current media accounts and information gleaned from several sources within the church, that more and more people are "calling her pastor" because her numbers are increasing, even as I write this. This is a phenomenon that will not go away, no matter how much resistance there is to women pastors. In fact, the actual instances in this book are merely the tip of the iceberg.

My solution is not to write a conclusion. Instead I will make some final observations about the following: (1) the creativity of women pastors in transforming constraints into opportunities; (2) recommendations for policy and for future research; and (3) the future of this new role for women, as seen by parishioners, priests, the women themselves, and this researcher.

TRANSFORMATION OF CONSTRAINTS

Constraints and opportunities are two threads that together form a theme running throughout this book. What is unique about the

167

women pastors is the way they manage to transform constraints into opportunities in the daily enactment of their new role.[1]

As I listened to my interviewees, and when I examined the transcripts, the word "challenge" emerged again and again. Phrases like, "taking on other challenges and more visionary things," "helping the church move into the future," "needing new challenges," "being a link between an older model of church and a brand new vision of what church can and should be," and "being challenged and stretched beyond what I thought I was capable of doing" kept recurring. One of the women pastors, for instance, said that she saw herself as taking part in a "pilot project" in her diocese, and she labeled the appointment of women as heads of parishes a "creative solution" to the priest shortage. In a real sense it was the very challenge of the constraints, conflicts, and tensions that attracted some of the women pastors to this new role.

What are some examples of the ways that these women managed to transform constraints into opportunities? A constraint that caused considerable tension, and that was mentioned repeatedly in the interviews with the women pastors, was their experience of rejection by parishioners, especially during the first few months following their arrival at the parish. Obviously the women pastors had somehow survived this initial rejection, because they were still in charge of the parish when I interviewed them, and had served in this capacity for an average of four years. In chapter 6 I discussed some of the support systems that helped them to overcome the "rejection period," but moral support and advice from others was not the only solution.

One of the priests described how a woman pastor transformed the parishioners' rejection of her into an opportunity. He said,

> One way she coped with it is she went to a workshop. I can't even tell you the title of it, but it was in that area of how to understand parishioners that reject you, not just because you are a woman but just reject what you do, and how you reach them. That's the way she is. This is another mountain she's got to climb and she'll climb it. She is a strong woman.

One of the initial experiences of these women, sometimes occurring the very first day they take over as pastor, is encountering parishioners who are anxious, fearful, or angry about losing their priest. Such people tend to bombard them with numerous questions that demand immediate answers. As I explained in chapter 6, bishops who traveled to the parish before the arrival of the new pastor fielded these questions themselves, thus saving the women pastors a considerable amount of time and energy. One of the lay pastors, who had previous pastoring experience in another parish, described her strategy:

> We had xeroxed and stapled together a cover letter to the parish along with ten or twelve commonly asked questions and answers about pastoral coordinators, and we had those mailed out to the whole parish mailing list that first week. And then we were up in the pulpit the first Sunday.

This tactic was successful because it enabled the copastors at this parish to lessen the time spent in explaining over and over again who they were and what they would be doing, and instead to get on with the work of the parish more easily.

One of the very sensitive issues which sometimes caused conflict within the parish and was a source of tension for many of the women pastors was their "right" to preach. The ambiguity surrounding this aspect of their role as pastor allowed some of them a certain degree of freedom. Several of the women pastors preached regularly, and because they knew the names of their parishioners and had visited their homes, they found new ways of reaching them in their sermons.

I observed this creativity when a woman pastor preached during a word and Communion service on a Sunday morning. She was interpreting the gospel for the day, the story of Zacchaeus, who, because he was short of stature, climbed a tree in order to see Jesus. In her introduction she explained that she, who was also short of stature, had walked around examining the trees on the parish grounds to see if she might be able to climb any of them, and had decided that she could not. She then immediately caught the attention of her audience by directly asking three very small boys who were sitting with their parents in the bench next to me, if they could climb a tree. She called on each one in turn by name, and asked, "Could you climb a tree?" And each one, with his eyes riveted on her face, replied, "No." She literally had these children and the entire congregation eating out of her hand.

She continued with an analogy, describing the actions of a young boy and girl who had to stand at a circus and because of their height couldn't see the performance. They cried, whined, and threw temper tantrums, yet refused help from their parents, and so missed seeing the show. She mentioned as a parallel, the actions of people who are failing in school or who are alcoholics and refuse help from others, thus compounding their problem. She then compared all of these examples to the actions of Zacchaeus who not only went out of his way to see Jesus, but also accepted the Lord's help and thus changed his life for the better. She kept saying to them throughout, "You can *do* it, but you need to accept help from others."

During this sermon, while making her point regarding the individual's need for community, she kept eye contact throughout, was very expressive, and did not use notes. And all of this was done within the confines of a religious service which is defined as "second class" because it was presided over by a nonordained minister who cannot celebrate Mass.[2]

Later, when this same woman pastor discussed what it is that keeps her going in her ministry, she included her opportunities to preach:

> I think the people [are what keeps me going in my ministry]. And an inner call. I really think the Spirit is the one that speaks through me, that is doing things on Sundays. I prepare because I really love preparing my Sunday liturgies as best as I can. Once I have it all written and all prepared, I say, "Lord, it is your job." And He/She takes over. I think it is that inner calling, the experienciang of the Lord in my life, and the people. I think they deserve more than what they have experienced in the past.

From what I observed and heard from my interviewees, the preaching done by these women was a key element in changing peoples' attitudes about women's role in the church. One of the priests, commenting on her homily, told a woman pastor that she had "sure rattled some cages." As she reiterated the conversation,

> I said, "Is that good or bad? What does that mean?" And he said, "Well, if you don't rattle cages, you don't open doors, do you?" So I said, "Thanks."

The doors begin to open when the parishioners perceive their woman pastor as someone who has assumed a seemingly incongruous position in their parish since her appearance and actions differ quite obviously from those of their previous pastors. It is difficult for people who had never previously seen a woman in such roles as pastor, Supreme Court justice, construction worker, soldier, or astronaut, to imagine such an eventuality. Such an image runs counter to individuals' experiences in everyday life.

However, most of the parishioners, who encounter their woman pastor on an almost daily basis, gradually come to the conclusion that she performs her pastoral duties as well as or better than the previous priest-pastor. As a result of these observations the "doors" of their imaginations have been opened to the possibility that SHE can do it, and do it effectively.

As we have seen in the previous chapters, these women are able to identify with their parishioners to a much greater extent than any previous pastor because they are not members of the clergy. Thus the constraints and limitations of their nonordained state are transformed into opportunities by their creation of a new leadership style that incorporates their parishioners as peers, and eventually leads to a greater spirit of community in these parishes.

Because Catholic parishioners share membership in the laity with their woman pastor, they are also keenly aware of the limitations placed on her authority, and they are beginning to question this inequity. An increase in parishioner questioning of the limited empowerment of women pastors is a signal that the doors are opening still wider. Thus institutional constraints actually are providing the opportunity for changes in attitude at the grass roots level.

RECOMMENDATIONS

Having traveled across the country to collect the data for this book, and having analyzed it in the previous pages, I am now prepared to present some recommendations that could make the transition into this new role a smoother one. The Catholic church is in the throes of an evolutionary change process which is experienced more profoundly in the poor and more isolated areas of the country at the present time. Any organization anticipating change should plan and prepare for it so as to be able to shape desirable outcomes.

One strategy that worked well in the parishes I visited was the active involvement of parishioners in the recruitment process. Some dioceses, in fact, have guidelines that require candidates to be interviewed by a committee of parishioners prior to the appointment by the bishop. As was shown in this study, it was not the status of nun or married woman, nor that of insider or outsider that necessarily made a "better pastor." It was rather the level of trust, which was enhanced by parishioner participation in the recruitment of the new lay pastor.

Other recommendations concern the role of the clergy in the legitimation of the newly appointed leader. The bishop should personally visit the parish prior to the arrival of the lay pastor to explain his reasons for alternate staffing, and he should also preside at the installation ceremony. He should appoint a priest-pastor as mentor for the lay pastor, at least for the first year. In addition, the bishop himself should visit the parish after the new pastor has been installed, so that he can periodically renew his support. Likewise, the priest acting as sacramental visitor should use every occasion to legitimize the authority of the lay pastor.

All of the strategies mentioned thus far also have obvious implications for secular organizations that are recruiting women into positions previously occupied by men.

It would certainly lighten the financial burdens in priestless parishes if the diocese would take on the responsibility of paying the stipend for the priest who performs the sacramental ministry. It does not seem fair that such a parish not only loses a resident priest, but also must incur a greater financial strain. In the interest of long-range planning, dioceses should fund scholarships to encourage laity to pursue master's programs in theology or pastoral studies. Perhaps seminaries and schools of theology could be persuaded to create scholarships for laity who are training for pastoral ministry.

Some recommendations regarding future research also come to mind. One of the central issues emerging from this study is the extent to which the patterns of behavior and attitude observed are due to the gender or to the lay status of the pastor. This issue can only be addressed with comparable data on male lay pastors.

However, at the present time, as I explained in chapter 1, there are only about twelve parishes in the United States headed by religious brothers, who, like sisters, are not ordained.[3] At the time that I drew my sample, there was only one married layman heading a priestless parish, and he is copastoring with his wife.[4] This points to the need for a study of male lay pastors of priestless parishes in the United States, so that we can make the basic gender comparisons.

As preceding chapters show, some evidence of bishops' support and nonsupport was gleaned from the interviews with women pastors, parishioners, and priests. What is needed now, however, is a research project focusing on the issue of alternate staffing of parishes that directly involves Catholic bishops. This proposed research would give us a better understanding of bishops' attitudes and behavior towards lay pastors.

Until the Catholic church allows ordination for women, there can be no direct comparisons with Protestant clergywomen. The women in my study lack the clerical privileges and rights that Protestant clergywomen possess; therefore their status is not comparable. Although many of the Catholic women pastors attested to the support of Protestant clergywomen in their local area, they were keenly aware of the difference in status.

Unlike Catholicism, which is experiencing continued growth in membership while the priesthood is shrinking, the mainline Protestant churches, with a surplus of clergy, are characterized by a declining membership.[5] Thus we cannot expect to see a similar phenomenon of increasing use of lay pastors in Protestant churches, at least in the foreseeable future.

My ethnographic research has given us a view of the behavior, perceptions, attitudes, and feelings of parishioners, women pastors, and priests in twenty parishes scattered throughout the United States that have no resident priest. This qualitative research should be complemented by a quantitative study with a national overview, which is already in progress. As I mentioned in chapter 1, a survey of parishes throughout the United States where there is no resident priest is now in preparation. It goes without saying that all of the research projects recommended above should also be extended to other countries throughout the world, so that cross-national comparisons could be made.

LOOKING TO THE FUTURE

What does the future look like to those who have experienced the pastoring of a woman in these parishes? Several of the priests who served with them as sacramental ministers offered serious reflections. One of them said,

> I really feel that these kinds of creative solutions are absolutely essential, not just because of the priest shortage. I think the grace part of the priest shortage is that it's allowing other ministries in the church to emerge. I think that's the gift from God...the shortage of priests. That other people, people who are not ordained, are in these kinds of roles is wonderful. And getting used to seeing a woman in that role is going to help visually for the day when finally God can break through in those places where it hasn't happened.

Parishioners also offered their views of the future. A woman parishioner who was in a diocese where the former bishop, who had appointed a woman pastor to head the parish, was recently retired, expressed some apprehension. She stated:

> From what I understand [the new bishop] is a little more strict about women's involvement and role in the church. For awhile there it gave us all a little bit of an uncomfortable, uneasy feeling about what the future was to hold. The possibility always is there that they could remove [her] or make a concerted effort to find a parish priest or bring in a deacon. So I think right now things are a little bit iffy, and I wonder if she is going to have the support of [the new bishop].

In several of the parishes I visited, women pastors, parishioners, and priests discussed the possibility of a rotation of priestless parishes, or "spreading it around." One of the parishioners put it this way:

> I had heard at a workshop that they were going to try working with these administrators [women pastors], to put as many as they can in the diocese to help the priests. They were talking

about moving priests around and putting administrators in the larger parishes, and giving everyone in the diocese a feel of having an administrator sometime or another. I would favor that kind of thing [rotation of priestless parishes]. I think people would feel more comfortable in the church, knowing that just because they are a small community, they would not always have a [lay] administrator.

The growing awareness by parishioners of the constraints and inequities faced by their woman pastors in carrying out their ministry led to another topic frequently mentioned by parishioners. This was the possibility of ordaining women. A male parishioner who was deeply concerned about the survival of the church phrased it this way:

> I think that whoever came up with this pastoral administrator job for the religious [women] and lay people should get into a position in our church that they would enlighten the view of our upper-echelon people. We have to do something. We are committing suicide. We just have to change. I feel we are wasting an awful lot of our resources. We should have ordination of women. It is just puzzling to me that we don't. People have to be protecting their own turf.

He continued with this same theme a little later in the interview:

> I just said a few minutes ago that we are committing suicide, and we are. We are losing members right and left, and we have no vision. In the Bible it says that Jesus founded this church and the gates of hell will not prevail against it. But I am afraid that we are prevailing against it, the members are.

What did the women pastors have to say about the future? Several of them had very practical recommendations, for example:

> I wish the church would wake up and start planning, not day to day. They keep putting Band-aids on situations, and now they have run out of Band-aids. I would love for them to look creatively at the diocese, places where they have mission churches and no community life—the people just use it as a place to go to church—[and] close them. To really study and see where community is, and to foster those communities of people.

Some of them offered carefully nuanced statements with regard to the ordination of women. One of the nun pastors stated that she "wouldn't want ordination to continue as it's been," adding that to ordain women in the current structure would mean having "a masculine structure with feminine bodies in it." She suggested a new, less hierarchical model of ordination that would reflect the more participatory style of leadership modeled by women pastors.

Similarly, a married pastor who always sat with the parishioners during Mass, and made it clear that she did not want to be placed on a clerical pedestal, said,

> If I were to sit in the presider's chair and do all those things, they [parishioners] would eventually do to me what they did to the priests. But I am always conscious that I want not only the sex to change, but the style of leadership to change. Even some people do this to me now, [saying] "Well, if you are not going to heaven, who is?" [I answer], "Just because I work in this position does not make me holier. You are just as holy as me. I could be a crook for all you know."

A nun pastor spoke of her dreams of the future church:

> I hope and pray, and keep wishing and dreaming that our church, especially our hierarchy, can open their eyes to the reality, and not continue burying their heads in the sand, [and] to face the reality with joy and optimism, and allow the lay people to really take over. If we are all baptized, and are all empowered, why can't we go ahead and minister completely? We would be more alive, more enriched. In one of the meetings I said, "I wish the Lord would come right now and tell us what He feels about our church, because we are massacring the whole thing." I wish we would open our eyes and our minds, and really allow the Spirit to do Her job.

As this study has shown, a change of parishioners' and priests' attitudes is already happening in parishes headed by women. I heard both laity and priests who were formerly opposed to women clergy describe their conversion. In the nine parishes headed by married women, this change of heart encompassed the issue of married clergy as well.

It is safe to say that the proportion of Catholics who have undergone this attitude change does not yet constitute a critical mass. At the present time there are only about two percent of the Catholic parishes in this country that have nonpriest pastors.

However, that percentage will increase as the priest shortage continues to become more critical. In increasing numbers the laity will be asking, "Why *not* women pastors?" and "Why *not* married pastors?"[6]

Whether this dramatic change in thinking will filter up to the hierarchy is not the question; it already has in some dioceses, and indications are that more and more bishops are appointing women to head parishes. Some dioceses that have enough priests at the present time will probably hold out for awhile, but by the year 2005, they will also experience the priest shortage, and will then have to decide whether to close parishes, import priests from other countries, or provide alternate staffing of them. It is my position that this slow but steady change in attitudes regarding women clergy and married clergy will, in the last analysis, portend well for the future of lay leadership in the church.

My prediction is, however, tempered by the awareness of the tendency to resist change, particularly on the part of those in positions of power. A striking example of the resistance to change came to my attention as this book was going to press. One of my interviewees, a woman who had been pastoring a parish for four years, wrote me a letter to inform me that she had been moved out of her parish by the bishop. Her replacement was a priest from a foreign country who, she wrote, "is destroying the beautiful community you witnessed there." She continued,

> And the bishop does *nothing* about it. For him the important thing is "having a priest in every parish," no matter what kind of a priest he is.

This is a clear reminder that institutional constraints cannot easily be transformed. It is also safe to predict that some bishops will opt for this type of alternate staffing, recruiting priests from other countries, instead of entrusting parishes to lay people. The notion of empowering the laity, even though supported by Vatican II decrees, runs counter to the Catholic tradition of hierarchical authority.[7] Those bishops who cling to that tradition will be more likely to go to great lengths to place a priest in every parish, no matter where he comes from. Such bishops will undoubtedly try to blind themselves to the problems caused in parishes led by pastors who are unfamiliar with the parishioners' language, values, and culture.

In this regard, the key issue is whether parishioners will continue to be submissive, and to accept the bishop's appointments unquestioningly. Some of them undoubtedly will continue to go along with all of the bishop's decisions, but there is evidence that the majority of American laity favor more democratic decision making at all three levels: parish, diocese, and Vatican.[8] Thus I predict that those bishops who appoint lay pastors to head parishes will continue to grow in number, until their decisions about alternate staffing of parishes will predominate in the early years of the third millenium.

Whether the movement toward greater lay participation will permeate the various offices at the Vatican is an open question. Unless the leader at the top accepts new roles for the laity, especially the inclusion of women in making decisions and shaping policy at the parish, diocesan, and Vatican levels, there is little hope for a restructuring that includes all levels of the Catholic church in the foreseeable future.

A significant obstacle to the appointment of lay pastors, which I discussed in chapter 7, is the financial one. How can poor parishes afford to pay them a living wage? This, of course, can only be answered on a parish-to-parish basis. However, most parishes that at one time had a resident priest own a parish house, and I would expect that many young laypersons interested in church ministry would find free housing a major asset. For example, the young couple who were copastors told me they were delighted to have a large parish house for themselves and their three children, and were well aware that most young couples their age could not afford such a home. Likewise, the laywoman and the nuns who were living in parish houses could not afford to accept the position without the rent-free housing.

Another financial solution is the "sharing" of a lay pastor by two parishes that together pay the salary. Still another solution, already experienced in almost all of the parishes I visited, is increased giving by the parishioners. As many parishioners told me, once they realized the benefits of having a woman pastor, they became actively engaged in the running of the parish. Thus the parishioners became part of the solution themselves, not only by their volunteer services, but also by contributing more to the Sunday collection.

There are some very poor parishes, however, with high unemployment rates, where contributing more money to the Sunday collection is not a possibility for the parishioners. There were a few parishes I visited that were able to raise money through annual bazaars and quilt sales, but this is less successful in a geographical area where the entire region is depressed. In such a case, wealthier parishes in the diocese could "adopt" the parish, and share their resources with them. Two of the parishes I visited were "adopted" parishes.

Poverty is not an insurmountable problem for pioneers, as we know from our own history as a nation. Needless to say, the image of the women and men who crossed this country in covered wagons includes few of the material comforts of life. These were poor but determined people who were risk-takers because they were in pursuit of a cherished dream. They were aware that they were participating in building the new nation that they had adopted.

The same can be said for these talented women pastors who are also encountering all of the obstacles that stand in the way of those who seek and accept the challenge of breaking new ground. Inspired by the Vatican II teaching that the church is the people of God, they are participating in the transformation of an institution of which they are an integral part. In parishes like those I visited throughout the country, the presence of women pastors is already beginning to change the face of Catholicism.

NOTES

CHAPTER 1

1. Although at the present time few dioceses in the Northeast have appointed nonordained persons to head parishes, Richard Schoenherr's recent research indicates that by the year 2005 dioceses in the New England region will decline most in the number of active diocesan priests, suffering an average loss of fifty-two percent between 1966 and 2005. See Richard A. Schoenherr and Lawrence A. Young, *The Catholic Priest in the United States: Demographic Investigations* (Madison, Wis.: University of Wisconsin-Madison Comparative Religious Organization Studies Publications, 1990), p. 23. Dolan et al. (1989:220) document an earlier period of leadership for women, prior to the establishment of parish programs. For instance, Mrs. John O'Brien was quite literally serving as pastor for twenty-five Catholics in Tallassee, Alabama in 1915. See also Weaver (1986:37–70).

2. The Roman Curia is the central administrative government of the Catholic church in Rome.

3. See Rosemary Ruether, *Contemporary Roman Catholicism: Crises and Challenges* (Kansas City, Mo.: Sheed and Ward, 1987), p. ix for a discussion of the meaning of *aggiornamento*.

4. See *Concilio Ecumenico Vaticano II: Commissioni Conciliari* for a list of the council participants.

5. See Walter M. Abbott, *The Documents of Vatican II* (New York: America Press, 1966), p. 500.

6. At that time I was one of the four American nuns invited to Rome by Cardinal Leon Joseph Suenens to organize discussions on topics that were on the current agenda of the Council.

7. No wonder, then, that Sister Teresa Kane's address to Pope John Paul II, on his visit to the United States in October, 1979 created such a sensation. She requested him to provide for women to be fully participating members of the church, and that they be included in all church ministries. See Dolan et al. (1989:189).

8. See Abbot (1966), p. 500. The term "apostolate" refers to the mission or activities of the church.

9. An abbess is a woman who is the superior of a convent of nuns.

10. See Joan Morris, *The Lady Was a Bishop* (New York: Macmillan, 1973), pp. 57, 75–77, and 85–86.

11. Some of this discussion is adapted from my earlier work on women in the church, in particular "Bringing Women In: Marginality in the Churches" (1975), "Catholic Women and the Creation of a new Social Reality" (1988), and "Women in the Church: Limited Empowerment" in D'Antonio, Davidson, Hoge, and Wallace (1989).

12. A eucharistic minister is a person who assists in the distribution of Communion. A lector is one who reads the scripture lessons during Mass or other liturgical celebrations.

13. David C. Leege and Thomas A. Trozzolo, "Who Participates in Local Church Communities?" *Origins* 15 (1985): 56–57.

14. William V. D'Antonio, James D. Davidson, Dean R. Hoge, and Ruth A. Wallace, *American Catholic Laity in a Changing Church* (Kansas City, Mo.: Sheed and Ward, 1989).

15. See William L. Baumgaertner, ed., *Fact Book on Theological Education: 1987–88* (Vandalia, Ohio: Association of Theological Schools in the United States and Canada, 1988), pp. 90–92.

16. In fact, some dioceses currently require that candidates for the position of pastoral administrator have already earned a master's degree in theology or its equivalent. Because only priests can have the title "pastor," these women are usually given the title "pastoral administrator" by their bishops.

17. See *Code of Canon Law* (Washington, D.C.: Canon Law Society of America, 1983).

18. See John A. Renken, "Canonical Issues in the Pastoral Care of Parishes without Priests," *The Jurist* 47 (1987): 506–19.

19. Ibid.

20. See Elaine Kroe, *National Higher Education Statistics: Fall 1989* (Washington, D.C.: U.S. Department of Education, 1989), pp. 11–13.

21. See Richard A. Schoenherr and Lawrence A. Young, *The Catholic Priest in the United States: Demographic Investigations* (Madison, Wis.: University of Wisconsin-Madison Comparative Religious

Organization Studies Publications, 1990). This exhaustive study was sponsored by the United States Catholic Conference.

22. Although Schoenherr's report did not include recommendations, Dean R. Hoge has suggested that the priesthood shortage would be alleviated if the laws regarding celibacy and male ordination were changed. See Dean R. Hoge, *The Future of Catholic Leadership: Responses to the Priest Shortage*, (Kansas City, Mo.: Sheed and Ward, 1987).

23. See Schoenherr and Young (1990), pp. 99–110.

24. Andrew M. Greeley, *American Catholics Since the Council: An Unauthorized Report* (Chicago: Thomas More Press, 1985), p. 182.

25. Hoge (1987). See also Kenneth L. Woodward, T. Stranger, S. Sullivan, M. Margolis and R. Vokey, "Church in Crisis," *Newsweek* (December 9, 1985): 66–75.

26. See *Origins* (December 17, 1979).

27. See Joseph H. Fichter, "Holy Father Church," *Commonweal* (May 15, 1970): 216–18.

28. The following are some examples: Matthew Clark, "American Catholic Women: Persistent Questions," *Origins* (1982) 12:273–86; Victor Balke and Raymond Lucker, "Male and Female God Created Them," *Origins* (1981) 11:333–38; and Peter Gerety, "Women in the Church," *Origins* (1980) 10:582–88.

29. A pastoral letter is the bishops' official guidance to American Catholics on how they should think about problems facing their church and their country. Previous pastorals have looked at such issues as the U.S. economy and nuclear arms.

30. See U.S. Bishops, "One in Christ Jesus: A Pastoral Response to the Concerns of Women for Church and Society," *Origins* 19 (1990): 717–40. See also Pat Windsor, "Weakland Advises U.S. Bishops to Drop Women's Pastoral," *National Catholic Reporter* (May 18, 1990:3), where it is reported that Milwaukee Archbishop Rembert Weakland advised the bishops not to issue this pastoral letter because it fails to mention the issue of power and decision making in the church, and how they are related to ordination. He predicted that until that relationship between ordination and jurisdiction is laid out clearly, "there will be no credible treatment of the role of women in the church. The gifts of women cannot be fully recognized if leadership roles have to be tied into ordination." A deacon is an ordained cleric ranking below a priest

who has the right to deliver homilies during Mass, and to preside at funerals and marriages outside of Mass.

31. See Daniel Pilarczyk, "Vote on Women's Pastoral Delayed," *Origins* 20 (September 27, 1990): 250–51.

32. See James A. Coriden, ed., *Sexism and Church Law: Equal Rights and Affirmative Action* (New York: Paulist Press, 1977), p. 159.

33. The term "nuns" historically refers to members of contemplative orders, and "sisters" denotes members of religious communities engaged in active ministries. However, modern usage tends to equate the two terms. In order to avoid any confusion with family relationships, I use the term nuns in most cases when I am referring to female members of religious communities.

34. See Peter Gilmour, *The Emerging Pastor: Non-ordained Catholic Pastors* (Kansas City, Mo.: Sheed and Ward, 1986). A sacramental minister is a priest, usually from a nearby parish, appointed to celebrate Mass and administer the other sacraments in parishes where there is no resident priest.

35. Professor Gary Burkart, chair of the Sociology Department at Benedictine College in Atchison, Kansas, is the principal investigator of this research project.

36. Totals ninety-nine percent because of rounding off percentages.

37. The data reported in the *Official Catholic Directory* are typically underreported, since they are compiled by the bishop's office in each diocese, and then sent to the publisher. Some bishops may be reluctant to admit that laity are administering their parishes, and instead list the priest who is the sacramental minister. For instance, I found five women whom I had interviewed in their parishes who were not listed as the administrator of the parish in the *Directory*. See *Origins* (April 19, 1990, Volume 19, No. 46: 758–65) for the full text of an address given on March 10, 1990 by H. Richard McCord, Jr., associate director of the National Conference of Catholic Bishops' Secretariat for Laity and Family Life, where he stated that already there are *at least* 201 pastoral administrators directing 193 parishes or missions in seventy dioceses in the United States.

38. See "Celibacy First, Eucharist Second," *Corpus Reports*, Vol. 16, No. 2 (March–April 1990): 3.

39. See Katherine Gilfeather, "The Changing Role of Women in the

Catholic Church in Chile," *Journal for the Scientific Study of Religion* 16 (1977): 53.

40. See Ruth A. Wallace, "Catholic Women and the Creation of a New Social Reality," *Gender and Society* 2 (1988): 24–38.

41. William V. D'Antonio et al., 1989.

42. For recent sociological studies of Protestant clergywomen, see Jackson W. Carroll, Barbara Hargrove, and Adair T. Lummis, *Women of the Cloth: A New Opportunity for the Churches* (San Francisco, Ca.: Harper and Row Publishers, 1983) and Edward C. Lehman, Jr., *Women Clergy: Breaking Through Gender Barriers* (New Brunswick, N.J.: Transaction Books, 1985).

43. I am especially indebted to Kay Seshkaitis, an expert on this topic, who was then working at the Office of Ministry for the Archdiocese of Portland, Oregon.

44. Here I draw on Robert Merton's work on role-sets. See Robert K. Merton, "The Role-Set: Problems in Sociological Theory," *British Journal of Sociology* 8 (1957: 106–20) and Robert K. Merton, *Social Theory and Social Structure* (New York: Free Press, 1968). The members of the woman pastor's role-set know that the individual who previously occupied her position was a member of the clergy, and his role performance was facilitated by a long tradition of clear-cut role expectations. Therefore I assumed that the members of her role-set would have different, and to some extent, indefinite or unclear role expectations. This is the reason why I wanted to concentrate on the role relationships between the woman pastor and the significant members of her role-set, the male and female parish leaders and the priest who was the sacramental minister for her parish.

45. My letter included two additional pieces of information: first, that the costs of my transportation, meals, and housing were covered by a grant from the Lilly Endowment; and second, in case they wished to check my references, I provided them with the names and addresses of three people in different parts of the country, all of whom are nationally known experts on aspects of pastoral ministry, who know me both professionally and personally.

46. A decrease in the numbers of Catholic women entering religious orders, and an increase in the numbers leaving, resulted in a total decrease of forty percent of the members of religious women's communities between 1966 and 1981. See Marie Augusta Neal, *Catholic Sisters in Transition: From the 1960s to the 1980s* (Wilmington, Del.: Michael Glazier, 1984), p. 19.

47. I combined New England and the Middle Atlantic to form the Northeast. The East North Central and West North Central were combined to form the Midwest. The South Atlantic, East South Central, and West South Central were combined to form the South. Finally, the West was a combination of the Mountain and Pacific regions.

48. Within the first hour of my arrival at each parish, before I began the first interview, I made it a point to describe some of my background to the women pastors, in particular the fact that I had spent eighteen years as a member of a religious community, and the rest (1970–present) as a laywoman. Thus I could identify with nuns and laywomen alike, and this commonality in backgrounds tended to "break the ice."

49. My research emphasizes the importance of the individual's interpretation of his or her situation, and the active employment of various strategies in order to manage one's behavior, thought, and feelings. Sociologists will recognize that symbolic interactionism is one of the key theoretical perspectives that informs this research. See Herbert Blumer, *Symbolic Interactionism: Perspective and Method* (Englewood Cliffs, N.J.: Prentice-Hall, 1969); Erving Goffman, *Presentation of Self in Everyday Life* (New York: Doubleday, 1959); George J. McCall and J. L. Simmons, *Identities and Interactions* (New York: Free Press, 1966); and Arlie Russell Hochschild, *The Managed Heart* (Berkeley: University of California, 1983) and *The Second Shift* (New York: Viking, 1989). Because I also emphasize the importance of institutional constraints and supports and demographic factors in an explanation of this phenomenon, this study is a combination of both micro and macro sociological analysis. See Anthony Giddens, *Central Problems in Social Theory* (Berkeley: University of California, 1983) and *The Constitution of Society* (Cambridge: Polity, 1984); and C. Wright Mills, *The Sociological Imagination* (New York: Oxford, 1959).

50. This restriction is contained in church law. Canons 150 and 521 state that the office of pastor requires the order of priesthood, and that it cannot be conferred on one who is not ordained to that order.

CHAPTER 2

1. Although there were no black women heading priestless parishes when I was collecting my data, a black nun was appointed to head a parish in Richmond, Virginia, and she assumed duties there on June 4, 1990. See Myra L. Dandridge, "Black Nun to Lead Parish in Virginia," *Washington Post* (May 26, 1990): D1.

2. Although both women and married persons are excluded from ordination to the priesthood, these restrictions do not apply in the case of pastoral administrators. As we saw in chapter 1, canon 517.2 did not exclude laity.

3. According to canon 766, laypersons can be permitted to preach in church in cases of necessity or usefulness.

4. A homily is a sermon presented to a congregation during Mass by a priest or deacon, usually after the scripture readings.

5. This appeared in the classified advertising section of the April 20, 1990 issue of the *National Catholic Reporter*, p. 21.

6. In a recent national study, Hoge et al. found the average size of Catholic parishes with no full-time clergy was 234 households (or families). See Dean R. Hoge, Jackson W. Carroll, and Francis K. Scheets, *Patterns of Parish Leadership: Cost and Effectiveness in Four Denominations* (Kansas City, Mo.: Sheed and Ward, 1988), p. 146. Therefore, my five "large" parishes would be interpreted as medium-size, and the rest would be labeled "small" on a national scale.

7. Myers-Briggs is the name of a personality inventory that is designed to characterize people on a number of psychological factors, one of which is introvert/extrovert.

CHAPTER 3

1. See *Webster's Ninth New Collegiate Dictionary* (Springfield, Ma.: Merriam-Webster, Inc., 1984), p. 861.

2. See *The Jerusalem Bible* (Garden City, N.Y.: Doubleday and Company, Inc., 1966), pp. 168–69.

3. A deanery is a geographical subdivision of a diocese comprising several parishes in a particular region, for example, a county.

4. In their study of the dying situation, Glaser and Strauss found that some nurses used strategies to avoid being near the patient during the later stages of dying because they found the death scene upsetting. See Barney G. Glaser and Anselm L. Strauss, *Awareness of Dying* (Chicago: Aldine Press, 1965), p. 202.

5. Robert Bellah defines community thus: "A group of people who are socially interdependent, who participate together in discussion and decision making, and who share certain practices that both define the

community and are nurtured by it. Such a community is not quickly formed. It almost always has a history and so is also a community of memory, defined in part by its past and its memory of its past." See Robert N. Bellah, Richard Madsen, William M. Sullivan, Ann Swidler, and Steven M. Tipton, *Habits of the Heart: Individualism and Commitment in American Life* (Berkeley: University of California Press, 1985), p. 333.

CHAPTER 4

1. See Doohan (1986:33–101) for a discussion of collaboration in parish ministry.

2. See, for instance, Emile Durkheim, *Suicide* (Glencoe, Ill.:Free Press, 1951), p. 156.

3. A missalette is a small book containing all that is said or sung at Mass.

CHAPTER 5

1. See Jay P. Dolan, R. Scott Appleby, Patricia Byrne, and Debra Campbell, *Transforming Parish Ministry: The Changing Roles of Catholic Clergy, Laity, and Women Religious* (New York: Crossroad, 1989), pp. 89–107, for a discussion of the emergence of the orchestra leader in contemporary parish life.

2. See Erving Goffman's *Presentation of Self in Everyday Life* (New York: Doubleday, 1959), pp. 106–40.

3. See Madeleine Adriance, *Opting for the Poor: Brazilian Catholicism in Transition* (Kansas City, Mo.: Sheed and Ward, 1986), p. 107.

4. Paulo Freire, *Pedagogy of the Oppressed* (New York: Seabury, 1970).

5. Neal recounts how the experience in base communities was the basis for transforming the forms of governance in women's religious communities. See Marie Augusta Neal, *From Nuns to Sisters: An Expanding Vocation* (Mystic, Conn.: Twenty-Third Publications, 1990), pp. 99–100.

CHAPTER 6

1. This chapter draws on role transition theory. See Vernon L. Allen and Evert van de Vliert, *Role Transitions: Explorations and Expla-*

nations (New York: Plenum, 1984), p. 3, who define role transition as "the process of changing from one set of expected positional behaviors in a social system to another."

2. I purposely wrote to the woman pastors for the invitation to visit the parish. Since they were in charge of the parish, I felt that this was the appropriate avenue. There were two reasons why I chose not to ask the bishop for either his permission or for the invitation. First, I feared that some bishops might refuse my request, thus eliminating those parishes from my sample. Second, if the bishop was the one who invited me to visit the parish, the woman pastor might be less than enthusiastic about having a researcher imposed on her by her bishop, with little or no say in the matter. Only on one occasion did I see the local bishop, who quite by accident happened to be a passenger on the same flight I was taking to his diocese. However, the woman pastor who met me at the airport quickly sized up the situation. After greeting the bishop, she very discreetly introduced me as "Dr. Ruth Wallace from George Washington University." Needless to say, a study of bishops' attitudes and behavior toward woman pastors is certainly in order, but this is beyond the purview of my research project.

3. The term "reflection talk" is sometimes used in order to avoid the word "homily," because church law denies laity the right to give homilies during Mass.

4. An alb is a full-length white linen vestment with long sleeves that is gathered at the waist with a cincture. This is worn by the priest officiating during Mass under the chasuble, a sleeveless outer vestment.

5. A newspaper article in the *Seattle Post-Intelligence* (May 19, 1990, p. A8) described a protest on the part of conservative Catholics against their bishop's stance on certain issues, including the following: "Using an alleged priest shortage to threaten practicing Catholics with priestless services and a denial of sacraments" to further the bishop's attempts to sanction women deacons and priests. In response the public affairs director for the diocese said that the bishop "believes women's rights is one of the most pressing issues confronting the church." Consequently the bishop canceled a training program for new deacons because he said "the church first should review the possibility of including women."

6. Chrism is consecrated oil used in the conferring of sacraments like baptism, confirmation, ordination, and the anointing of the sick.

7. CCD is the Confraternity of Christian Doctrine, the religious education program in the parish.

8. The vicar general is an administrative deputy of a bishop with authority second only to that of the diocesan bishop.

9. Shortly after I completed the data collection phase of this study, I traveled to Kansas City to meet with the director of the Institute for Pastoral Life, Jean Marie Hiesberger. I spent one morning with her and the members of her staff, conferring with them about topics for future programs sponsored by the Institute, and about the plans for their national survey of lay pastors.

10. The chief drawback of this program is that the funding is earmarked for poor rural parishes; therefore, women who are heading urban parishes would have to depend on their parish or diocese to cover the travel and housing costs. The material presented also would have to be expanded or adapted to cover issues peculiar to urban parishes.

CHAPTER 7

1. This chapter draws on the structuration theory of Anthony Giddens, who argues that structure is both enabling and constraining. In his book, *Central Problems in Social Theory* (Berkeley: University of California, 1983), p. 71, Giddens states: "According to the notion of the duality of structure, rules (or constraints) and resources are drawn upon by actors in the production of interaction, but are thereby also reconstituted through such interaction."

2. On the recommendation of the National Council of Catholic Bishops, a local bishop may request permission from the Vatican to delegate a layperson to witness a wedding. Archbishop Francis Hurley received the authorization in January 1990, and appointed six parish administrators—five nuns and one laywoman—as witnesses of Catholic weddings in the Archdiocese of Anchorage, Alaska. See *Origins* (February 15, 1990): 598.

3. Richard A. Schoenherr, "Power and Authority in Organized Religion," *Sociological Analysis* 47 (1987:68) argues that a variety of approaches is needed in order to have a better understanding of changing beliefs and shifting power in organized religion.

4. A penitential service is a preparatory ritual for the sacrament of confession.

5. A "dry Mass" literally means a "practice Mass" where a deacon who is about to be ordained a priest "goes through the motions," as it

were. What this woman meant was that she would simply distribute Communion after the homily if the priest did not appear.

CHAPTER 8

1. See Nijole V. Benokraitis and Joe R. Feagin, *Modern Sexism* (Englewood Cliffs, N.J.: Prentice-Hall, 1986) for numerous examples of both overt and covert sex discrimination in male-dominated occupations.

2. See for instance, Christine L. Williams, *Gender Differences at Work: Women and Men in Nontraditional Occupations* (Berkeley, Calif.: University at California Press, 1989).

3. Rosabeth Moss Kanter, *Men and Women of the Corporation* (New York: Basic Books, 1977) discusses the phenomenon of "solo hires," women who have the experience of being "tokens" in work settings in large corporations.

4. See Arlie Russell Hochschild, *The Second Shift: Working Parents and the Revolution at Home* (New York: Viking, 1989).

5. A lectionary is a book of biblical readings used in the liturgy.

CHAPTER 9

1. Giddens (1983:91–93) argues that individuals possess a transformative capacity because they can intervene in events in the world, and by their utilization of resources, produce definite outcomes.

2. In Giddens's (1983:88) view, this exemplifies the way that social transformations take place through innovative practices or "strategic conduct," to use his term.

3. One of the reasons why there are so few male lay pastors is that the majority of Catholic men who desire pastoral ministry are practicing it as priests. According to the 1990 *Official Catholic Directory,* there are 6,743 brothers in the United States, a three percent decrease from the previous year. This is a higher decrease than that of sisters, who now number 103,269, a one percent decrease from 1989.

4. Technically, deacons should not be classified as male lay pastors, because they are members of the clergy. Whether their perceived identity is lay or clerical, however, is not clear.

5. Schoenherr and Young call the Catholic situation the "dilemma of full pews and vacant altars." See Richard A. Schoenherr and Lawrence A. Young, "Quitting the Clergy: Resignations in the Roman Catholic Priesthood," *Journal for the Scientific Study of Religion* 29 (1990): 464.

6. Most Catholics are unaware that there are already married priests ministering with ecclesiastical approval in the United States. On May 20, 1989 the forty-second married Episcopal priest was ordained to the Catholic priesthood by Cardinal O'Connor in New York. See Joseph Fichter's study of this phenomenon in his book, *The Pastoral Provisions: Married Catholic Priests* (Kansas City, Mo.: Sheed and Ward, 1989), p. 1.

7. See, for instance, John Seidler and Katherine Meyer, *Conflict and Change in the Catholic Church* (New Brunswick,N.J.: Rutgers University Press, 1989), pp.158–68.

8. See D'Antonio et al. (1989:108–14).

BIBLIOGRAPHY

Abbott, Walter M. *The Documents of Vatican II*. New York: America Press, 1966.

Adriance, Madeleine. *Opting for the Poor: Brazilian Catholicism in Transition*. Kansas City, Mo.: Sheed and Ward, 1986.

Allen, Vernon L., and Evert van de Vliert, eds. *Role Transitions: Explorations and Explanations*. New York: Plenum Press, 1984.

Baumgaertner, William L., ed. *Fact Book on Theological Education: 1987–88*. Vandalia, Ohio: Association of Theological Schools in the United States and Canada, 1988.

Bellah, Robert N., Richard Madsen, William M. Sullivan, Ann Swidler, and Steven M. Tipton. *Habits of the Heart: Individualism and Commitment in American Life*. Berkeley: University of California Press, 1985.

Benokraitis, Nijole V., and Joe R. Feagin. *Modern Sexism: Blatant, Subtle, and Covert Discrimination*. Englewood Cliffs, N.J.: Prentice-Hall, 1986.

Biddle, B. J. "Recent Developments in Role Theory." *Annual Review of Sociology* 12 (1986): 67–92.

Blumer, Herbert. *Symbolic Interactionism: Perspective and Method*. Englewood Cliffs, N.J.: Prentice-Hall, 1969.

Bock, E. Wilber. "The Female Clergy: A Case of Professional Marginality." *American Journal of Sociology* 27 (1967): 531–39.

Burr, W. R. "Role Transitions: A Reformulation of Theory." *Journal of Marriage and the Family* 34 (1972): 406–16.

Carroll, Jackson W., Barbara Hargrove, and Adair T. Lummis. *Women of the Cloth: A New Opportunity for the Churches*. San Francisco, Calif.: Harper and Row, 1983.

Concilio Ecumenico Vaticano II: Commissioni Conciliari. Vatican City: Polyglot Press, 1965.

Coriden, James A., ed. *Sexism and Church Law: Equal Rights and Affirmative Action*. New York: Paulist Press, 1977.

Dandridge, Myra L. "Black Nun to Lead Parish in Virginia." *Washington Post* (May 26, 1990): D1.

D'Antonio, William V., James D. Davidson, Dean R. Hoge, and Ruth A. Wallace. *American Catholic Laity in a Changing Church*. Kansas City, Mo.: Sheed and Ward, 1989.

Dolan, Jay P., R. Scott Appleby, Patricia Byrne, and Debra Campbell. *Transforming Parish Ministry: The Changing Roles of Catholic Clergy, Laity, and Women Religious*. New York: Crossroad, 1989.

Doohan, Leonard. *Grass Roots Pastors: A Handbook for Career Lay Ministers*. San Francisco: Harper and Row, 1986.

Durkheim, Emile. *Suicide*. Glencoe, Ill.: Free Press, 1951.

Fichter, Joseph H. *The Pastoral Provisions: Married Catholic Priests*. Kansas City, Mo.: Sheed and Ward, 1989.

———. "Holy Father Church." *Commonweal* (May 15, 1970): 216–18.

Freire, Paulo. *Pedagogy of the Oppressed*. New York: Seabury Press, 1970.

Giddens, Anthony. *Central Problems in Social Theory*. Berkeley: University of California Press, 1983.

———. *The Constitution of Society*. Cambridge: Polity Press, 1984.

Gilfeather, Katherine. "The Changing Role of Women in the Catholic Church in Chile." *Journal for the Scientific Study of Religion* 16 (1977): 39–54.

Gilmour, Peter. *The Emerging Pastor: Non-ordained Catholic Pastors*. Kansas City, Mo.: Sheed and Ward, 1986.

Glaser, Barney G., and Anselm L. Strauss. *Awareness of Dying*. Chicago: Aldine Press, 1965.

Goffman, Erving. *Presentation of Self in Everyday Life*. New York: Doubleday, 1959.

Greeley, Andrew M. *American Catholics Since the Council: An Unauthorized Report*. Chicago: Thomas More Press, 1985.

Hochschild, Arlie Russell. *The Managed Heart: Commercialization of Human Feeling*. Berkeley: University of California Press, 1983.

———. *The Second Shift: Working Parents and the Revolution at Home*. New York: Viking, 1989.

Hoge, Dean R. *The Future of Catholic Leadership: Responses to the Priest Shortage.* Kansas City, Mo.: Sheed and Ward, 1987.

Hoge, Dean R., Jackson W. Carroll, and Francis K. Scheets. *Patterns of Parish Leadership: Cost and Effectiveness in Four Denominations.* Kansas City, Mo.: Sheed and Ward, 1988.

Hurley, Francis. "Authorization Received for Lay Witnesses of Weddings." *Origins* 19.37 (February 15, 1990):597–99.

John Paul II. *Code of Canon Law.* Washington, D.C.: Canon Law Society of America, 1983.

Kanter, Rosabeth Moss. *Men and Women of the Corporation.* New York: Basic Books, 1977.

Kennedy, Eugene. *Tomorrow's Catholics Yesterday's Church: The Two Cultures of American Catholicism.* San Francisco: Harper and Row, 1990.

Kroe, Elaine. *National Higher Education Statistics: Fall 1989.* Washington, D.C.: U.S. Department of Education, 1989.

Leege, David C., and Thomas A. Trozzolo. "Who Participates in Local Church Communities?" *Origins* 15 (1985): 56–57.

Lehman, Edward C. *Women Clergy: Breaking through Gender Barriers.* New Brunswick, N.J.: Transaction Books, 1985.

McCall, George J., and J. L. Simmons. *Identities and Interactions.* New York: The Free Press, 1966.

Merton, Robert K. "The Role-Set: Problems in Sociological Theory." *British Journal of Sociology* 8 (1957) 106–20.

———. *Social Theory and Social Structure.* New York: The Free Press, 1968.

Mills, C. Wright. *The Sociological Imagination.* New York: Oxford University Press, 1959.

Morris, Joan. *The Lady Was a Bishop.* New York:Macmillan, 1973.

Neal, Marie Augusta. *Catholic Sisters in Transition: From the 1960s to the 1980s.* Wilmington, Del.: Michael Glazier, 1984.

———. *From Nuns to Sisters: An Expanding Vocation.* Mystic, Conn.: Twenty-Third Publications, 1990.

Pilarczyk, Daniel. "Vote on Women's Pastoral Delayed." *Origins* 20 (September 27, 1990) 250–51.

Renken, John A. "Canonical Issues in the Pastoral Care of Parishes without Priests." *The Jurist* 47 (1987) 506–19.

Report of Catholic Biblical Association. *Origins* (December 17, 1979).

Rosenberg, Florence, and Edward M. Sullivan. *Women and Ministry: A Survey of the Experience of Roman Catholic Women in the United States.* Washington, D.C.: Center for Applied Research in the Apostolate, 1980.

Ruether, Rosemary Radford. *Contemporary Roman Catholicism: Crises and Challenges.* Kansas City, Mo.: Sheed and Ward, 1987.

Schoenherr, Richard A. "Power and Authority in Organized Religion: Disaggregating the Phenomenological Core." *Sociological Analysis* 47 (March 1987): 52–71.

Schoenherr, Richard A., and Lawrence A. Young. *The Catholic Priest in the United States: Demographic Investigations.* Madison, Wis.: University of Wisconsin-Madison Comparative Religious Organization Studies Publications, 1990.

———. "Quitting the Clergy: Resignations in the Roman Catholic Priesthood." *Journal for the Scientific Study of Religion* 29 (1990): 463–481.

Seidler, John, and Katherine Meyer. *Conflict and Change in the Catholic Church.* New Brunswick, N.J.: Rutgers University Press, 1989.

The Jerusalem Bible. Garden City, N.Y.: Doubleday, 1966.

The Official Catholic Directory. New York: Kenedy, 1990.

U.S. Bishops. "One in Christ Jesus: A Pastoral Response to the Concerns of Women for Church and Society." *Origins* 19 (1990): 717–40.

Wallace, Ruth A. "Bringing Women In: Marginality in the Churches." *Sociological Analysis* 34 (1975): 3–11.

———. "Catholic Women and the Creation of a New Social Reality." *Gender and Society* 2 (1988): 24–38.

Weaver, Mary Jo. *New Catholic Women: A Contemporary Challenge to Traditional Religious Authority.* San Francisco: Harper and Row, 1986.

Webster's Ninth New Collegiate Dictionary. Springfield, Mass.: Merriam-Webster, Inc., 1984.

Windsor, Pat. "Weakland Advises U.S. Bishops to Drop Women's Pastoral." *National Catholic Reporter* (May 18, 1990): 3.

Wittberg, Patricia. "Non-Ordained Workers in the Catholic Church: Power and Mobility Among American Nuns." *Journal for the Scientific Study of Religion* 28.2 (1989): 148–61.

Woodward, Kenneth L., T. Stranger, S. Sullivan, M. Margolis, and R. Vokey. "Church in Crisis." *Newsweek* (December 9, 1985): 66–75.

INDEX

Aaron's Blessing, 65
Abbesses, 4, def. 182n.9
Abrazo, 63
Absolution, 135, 143
Aggiornamento, 2, 87
Alb, 120, 130, 131, 164, def. 189n.4
Altar, 43, 60, 64, 94, 114, 118, 130;
    parishioners bothered by woman
    on, 141, 160; priest who does not
    allow women on, 133, 135, 136;
    priest who supports women on,
    116; women on altar a mortal sin,
    8; altar server, 5, 8, 51, 90, 96, 130,
    157
Altar and Rosary Society, 96, 161
Alternate staffing, 27, 77, 103, 105,
    106, 160, 172, 177, 178; foreign
    priest, 31, 33, 74, 177
Anchorage, Archdiocese of, 32
Anoint, 143; anointing the sick, 189
Anomie, 144
Appointment, 8, 14, 19, 34, 102, 117,
    168, 178; actions prior to, 17, 32,
    42, 49, 68, 69, 74, 78, 100, 116, 172;
    contract, 76, 109, 110, 147; follow-
    ing, 29-30, 55, 63, 107; insider, 33,
    35-36, 74, 77, 88; interviewing with
    parish committee, 34, 172
Appreciation Day, 51, 93
Approachable, 43, 44
Approval, 107, 108, 111
Apostolate, 4, 143, def. 181n.8
Attendance, 8, 81, 120, 121, 158;
    attend Mass at another church, 17
Authority, 67, 73, 75, 79, 139, 177; cir-
    cular, 85, 88, 91, 100; recognizing,
    109, 172; undermining, 113, 140,
    153, 171
Auxiliary role, 127

Balancing, 134
Base community, *See* Basic Ecclesial
    Communities
Basic ecclesial communities, 99, 100,
    104, 188n.5
Birth, 122, 152
Blessed Virgin Mary, 152
Budget, 96, 140
Burnout, 140

Canon 517.2, 7, 8, 187n.2; canon law
    revision, 7; canon lawyers, 6, 7, 9,
    13; Code of Canon Law, 6, 7, 8, 12,
    186
Castillo Lara, Archbishop Rosalio Jose,
    7
Catholic Biblical Association of Ameri-
    ca, 10
Celebrity, 152
Cemetery, 52, 82, 83, 103, 111, 118
Chancellors, 6, 9, 13
Charisma, 30
Chasuble, 130, def. 189n.4
Chauvinist, 155
Children, 114; caring for, 48-49; recog-
    nizing, 51; teaching, 95, 110, 137,
    169; taking drugs, 64; getting preg-
    nant, 64; women administrators
    with, 22, 39, 68, 118, 178
Chile, 13
Clergy, 6, 9, 151, 157, 172; nuns' rela-
    tionships to, 4, 16, 101; compare to
    Protestant, 129, 173; clergy educa-
    tion, 103; laity's relationship to, 6,
    87-89, 90, 126, 171; shortage, 54,
    73, 98, support of women's ordina-
    tion, 10, 176-77; *See also* Laity,
    Priest Shortage
Clerical collar, 129